T W I N
from Another Tribe

T W I N
from Another Tribe

The Story of Two Shamanic Healers
from Africa and North America

■ ■ ■ ■ ■

Michael Ortiz Hill
and
Mandaza Augustine Kandemwa

▼ ▼ ▼ ▼ ▼

A publication supported by
THE KERN FOUNDATION

Quest Books
Theosophical Publishing House

Wheaton, Illinois ♦ Chennai (Madras), India

Quest Books
The Theosophical Publishing House
PO Box 270
Wheaton, IL 60189-0270

www.questbooks.net

Cover art: José Ortega/Images.com

Cover design, book design, and typesetting by Beth Hansen-Winter

Library of Congress Cataloging-in-Publication Data

Hill, Michael Ortiz.

Twin from another tribe: the story of two Shamanic healers from Africa and North America / Michael Ortiz Hill and Mandaza Augustine Kandemwa.—1st Quest ed.

p.   cm.

ISBN-13: 978-0-8356-0852-7

ISBN-10: 0-8356-0852-2

1. Spiritual healing. 2. Shamanism—Africa. 3. Shamanism—United States. 4. Kandemwa, Mandaza Augustine. 5. Hill, Michael Ortiz 6. Shamans—Africa—Biography. 7. Shamans—United States—Biography. I. Kandemwa, Mandaza Augustine. II. Title.

BL65.M4H55 2007

201'.440922—dc22

[B]

2006019987

5   4   3   2   1   *   07   08   09   10   11

Printed in the United States of America

CONTENTS

CONCLUSION

EPILOGUE

AFTERWORD *by Deena Metzger*

ACKNOWLEDGMENTS

In Africa, a ritual circumstance such as this one begins by thanking the ancestors.

My father, Milford Lee Hill, was a child in Alamogordo, New Mexico, his heart ensnared by revival tents and a narrow strand of Christianity. It was then that he read a "Superman" comic book advertising a different way of the sacred. The Theosophists extended the thread that led him into the passions of learning about the world's religions and their histories and pathways. It was that comic book that led him to the East and elsewhere, intellectually and spiritually, to cultivate a wide field.

The last few years of my father's life I aspired to such a field as only a teenager can when he's in that long spasm of creating himself within a terrified and hopeful heart. While my father's health failed, I returned to his library as a holy place—like him, a high school dropout and, like him, a vagrant soul. Sitting among his books, I was sitting in the circle of the ancestors.

Because of those years of listening, I share his radically pluralistic view of sacred culture and his intrigue with the languages with which different peoples understand "the Way." I do not exaggerate that this early cooking made it ultimately possible for me to step across the epistemological frontier and be initiated as a healer in tribal Africa.

So I pay homage to my father, but homage also to the anonymous and prescient Theosophist who decided to seed the souls of boys with longing for the sacred between the pages of "Superman." My life has been shaped by that inspired moment of crazy wisdom.

I write this, of course, with great affection and humor, because Superman himself apparently delivered this vagrant son of a vagrant son to this Theosophical/Quest edition of this memoir of black and white twins.

Gratitude to Sharron Dorr, who saw the possibilities of what was once *Gathering in the Names,* and much gratitude to Carolyn Bond, editor extraordinaire, who with great care and warmth helped me pull out and extend the story within the story.

Both Carolyn and Sharron carried my psyche in ways they will never know. Midway through the long labor, I was pulled far downstream by a prescribed medication that makes for a touch of madness. Between Sharron noting that I was working on this book about healing in the middle of a healing crisis and Carolyn helping me to craft and recraft the story even as I was being recrafted, what can I possibly say?

Publishers and editors like this don't grow on every bush.

Gratitude, also, to my wife Deena Metzger, who these twenty years has accompanied me across many thresholds. As I write these words, she is in Idaho, with the bear and deer on the ground and above her the Northern Lights. She will be alone for forty-nine days.

Thresholds upon thresholds upon thresholds. Deena accompanied me through the necessary breakdowns that made it possible to be a healer.

Gratitude, as well, to Simakuhle Kandemwa, Mandaza's wife, who after some initial fear came to trust me and invited me to be with her Zulu ancestors. Bless her beauty, her elegance, and her loving heart.

Gratitude to those of so many tribes who drum and sing at our community in Bulawayo, Zimbabwe. I am honored to have been trusted even as the horror of apartheid was among them. In receiving this white stranger as family, they have taught me so much about healing.

And gratitude to Jim Devereaux, who has carried Africa in his heart since Mandaza and I initiated him almost ten years ago. When famine swept over Zimbabwe in the late nineties, we gathered and distributed resources. To keep school fees available, food on the table, and medical emergencies met were jobs I most certainly couldn't have done alone. Jim was impeccable and committed against unbearable circumstances and endless roiling and unraveling frustration. *Notenda*, Jim.

Thank you.

Gratitude to the people and the *daré* communities in North America that have kept the African worlds alive during this time of crisis. *Daré* is the Shona word for "council," that vibrant configuration that Deena Metzger writes about in the afterword. It is believed that whenever the living gather in a circle the ancestors are also among them, so *daré* refers to a council of the invisibles as well as of people.

Gratitude specifically to the *daré* in Topanga, California that received me and made a home for me in my very home, perplexed as I was about how to span Zimbabwe and America.

Gratitude to Chuck Madansky and Wilderness Sarchild, who founded the Cape Cod *daré*, for their courage in taking up the labor that Jim and I had so long maintained. Their Tatenda non-profit is a thing of beauty and necessity, as hunger still gnaws at central Africa.

Finally, homage to Musikavanhu, Tsitsi Hougabook, and Reverend Merikara of the KRST Unity Center for African Spirituality. Years before I met Mandaza, I had seen the connection between African-American nightly dreams and the Motherland: black Americans dream in "African." More than any others, these three people have made a home for Mandaza among black Americans. They have made it possible for him to come to that place in America where history and redemption meet. The Hebrew word is *tikkun olam*—gathering the sparks of the body of God shattered by history.

In this the world begins to mend.

Thank you for your persistence.

Thank you.

Michael Ortiz Hill
Topanga, California, 2006

INTRODUCTION

*Whenever two or more of you
are gathered in my name,
there I am among you.*

—Matthew 18:20

■ ■ ■ ■ ■

BLACK TWIN, WHITE TWIN

MICHAEL: This book is about peacemaking and healing by two initiates in the healing and peacemaking tradition that lies at the headwaters of African-American culture: the Bantu tradition of the water spirits. It is about shamanic initiation and the alliance with Spirit and spirits that the shaman relies on to do healing. It is about sacred illness and sacred healing. It is about living the shamanic life in the modern world among the poor in Africa and in an American teaching hospital. It is about the borderland between Western medicine and shamanic practices. It is about living the life of compassion and the stripping down to the elemental truth of oneself that makes such a life possible. It is about the blessed vulnerability of meeting the "enemy" as friend and teacher. It is about all of these things within the memoirs of a black man and a white man who recognize each other as twin.

The story of the twins was born of blood and fire. Mandaza came of age into civil war in Africa, the black majority rising up against the brutal white colonial government: Rhodesia in the sixties and seventies. For myself, a biracial white boy of Mexican descent, coming of age was about racialized anguish: the mean streets of New Mexico and, ultimately, Los Angeles on fire.

Blood and fire. 1992. Four white policemen caught on videotape viciously beating a black motorist yet acquitted by an all-white jury. For days the streets were filled with enraged Angelenos. Some called it riot, some called it uprising; for myself, it was simply heartbreak.

All my life I had lived within the insanity of race. I had just published my first book, *Dreaming the End of the World,* about the geography of apocalypse as revealed in apocalyptic dreams. I began to wonder: What might white and black people's dreams about each other tell us about the geography of race, that subterranean and unspoken world within and beneath every American city? I began collecting dreams.

So begins one way of telling the story of how the twins came to recognize each other, in fact, a very Western way. Blood and fire—are we not, if we tell the truth, all born of blood and fire? Blood and fire and the anguish of history. The tears of ethical choice, the ravaged heart of a young man who desires to be a peacemaker and healer—he responds by re-searching a book on dreams.

Why do I call this a Western way of telling the story? In Africa it is said that God speaks the story of our life. The truer story is born of the Incomprehensible and lived in relationship to the Mystery, and when we are initiated and when we die we relent fully to the Mystery that gave us birth.

I must say that before I was called to Africa for the sake of peacemaking I had no special attraction to African spiritual-ity. My ignorance was fully equal to the ignorance of most people in the Europeanized world. Africa remained fully the "dark continent," teeming with (presumably) noble savages. I knew nothing and was ignorant enough to not know how very ignorant I was.

I was raised Catholic but was also raised within my Bud-dhist father's library: Dogen Zenji, D. T. Suzuki, Alan Watts, Krishnamurti, Annie Besant, and *The Tibetan Book of the Dead.* Sri Aurobindo and *The Collected Works of C. G. Jung.* The Tao Te Ching and the Bhagavad Gita. These texts conveyed the voices of the elders. These *were* the ancestors. By the time I was a young man I had a passing acquaintance with the "civilized" world's religions, with a special interest in the monastic, the contemplative, and the mystical.

As a teenager I began to practice Buddhism, the rigor of returning again and again to silence. The quiet lucidity of Soto Zen remains my spiritual practice.

Not very African.

I was drawn to my twin not through spirituality but on a current of dreams.

As the ashes of the riot or uprising dampened with the winter rains I was deep in looking at the patterns in African-American dreams and trying to understand the scholarship on the origins of black American culture. My psyche was split open, and every night I dreamt blacks, dreamt Africa. In the days I reflected on my long history with African-Americans and my gratitude and confusion.

It was then that I first dreamt Mandaza, though at the time I didn't know it was he. An African man pointed to an unseen presence in a corner of his room and observed, "She says, congratulations, you have made it. It was very hard to get here but you are home now."

It would be four very hard years before I met Mandaza and he said those very words.

Upon hearing them, I knew I was indeed home.

The first afternoon we were together, Mandaza told me that, in his own dream, he had searched the hills of the holy land of Matopos looking for his white brother, and his wife, Simakuhle, had dreamt that one of the sons of the family would soon return. When I suggested to Mandaza that our ancestors seemed to be getting acquainted, he said, "Oh no. They have known each other since before we were born. They arranged this meeting."

The following day we began initiating each other, calling each other forth. This mystery of mutual initiation seems to be the way two shamans work when they see each other as twins. It was very much a surprise to both of us!

Who are they, these spirits?

Contrary to old fantasies of "primitive" and "heathen," tribal Africans are profoundly monotheistic. And yet for them the world is also inspirited, rich with spirits that mediate the sacred.

In one variation or another, this is the common belief from culture to culture the world over. The poetry of the One and the Many describes the rainbow that is the human tribe.

In Christianity, Christ mediates. Catholicism has its saints, Judaism has its angels, and in Islam the ninety-nine names of God bridge the gap from the Nameless One to us, the named. In the Immaculate Oneness of the Enlightened Mind, the Buddhist Heart Sutra chants: "Form is Emptiness, Emptiness is Form." The numerous Bodhisattvas draw the mind to utter Presence.

The community of spirits that Mandaza and I serve are called *midzimu* by his people, the Shona. Usually *midzimu* is translated as "ancestor," which is accurate enough if one understands that in Africa ancestors are not merely genealogical, not merely a matter of bloodline, race, DNA, or even species. Ambuya Bwebwe, Grandmother Spider, is a *midzimu* to which Mandaza and I are intimately grateful. Mandlovu, the Elephant, has shaped our fate. These two come through in the activities of healing and make family and community across cultural and racial lines possible.

Like the Holy Spirit that possesses a Pentacostal who speaks in tongues, like Christ appearing to St. Francis in the form of a leper, like Manjusri the Bodhisattva, fierce and precise with his sword that cuts through the delusive mind, the *midzimu* are Invisibles. Yes, this particular spider here, that elephant over there bear flesh and beauty, but the spirits of Spider and Elephant are met in initiation when one finds one's way into the village of the *midzimu.* They call, one answers and makes alliances. They come again and again in the daily life of the *nganga,* as a shaman is called.

For an initiated healer the Divine lives in the activity of healing. "Let me be God's hands!" prays Mandaza. In the Bantu languages, *God* is most certainly a verb. Not "Spirit" but the movement of Spirit. Not "spirits" but the activity of the *midzimu.*

The ritual tradition that Mandaza initiated me into, the *ngoma* (tradition) of the water spirits, is what anthropologists call a cult of affliction. The water spirits are the oldest layer of the ancestral world, long preceding the arrival of humans. Mandaza, quite literate in Christianity because of his missionary education under apartheid, says these spirits were born when the wind of God spread across the endless waters at the beginning: Genesis. They are the spirits closest to God, and they call the hapless to the practice of healing through sacred disease. The only cure for water spirit illness is initiation. Much of this book speaks of the twins being undone in Africa and America by sacred illness and being healed by reconciliation with the spirits that caused the illness. This reconciliation is one way to describe the initiation of a healer.

Initiation is commonly understood as an induction into a new society or state of being by special rites and ceremonies.

In the African tradition, the initiation to become a healer is about reconciliation with Spirit so one's whole life might be hospitable to Spirit, so one's life might be a vehicle for Spirit in healing an anguished world. The Africans believe that it is not other people who are guiding the initiate, but the spirits. Other people simply mediate; and, in this ritual tradition, the initiate himself learns to become a mediator between the spirit world and the human world—or "the village," as the Africans put it.

In this initiatory process, the *nganga* is the mediator. She or he relies on prayers, an implicit trust in Spirit, the old songs, an attentive ear to the initiate's dreams, a ritual imagination and a feeling heart to help cut the path for the initiate to find an authentic life of service. All cultures bear shadows. In America the shadow seems to be narcissism, the blind greed of "me first." In Africa one is initiated for the sake of the world.

Several years before I met Mandaza, I stumbled onto the underground connection between Africa and America in the dream life of black Americans. In the introduction to my book *The Village of the Water Spirits* (Spring Press, 2006), in which Mandaza helps me understand black people's dreams about white people, I write of the night I began seeing African patterns in the dreams of a Mr. Cary, a prisoner incarcerated in upstate New York.

That long night I was riven with astonishment and perplexity as I shuffled between dreams and sheaves of xeroxed manuscripts on Bantu culture, and although I could not grasp the implications it was irrefutable that Mr. Cary was dreaming whites in exactly the same fashion that Bantu people have understood whiteness since the Portuguese first made contact with the kingdom of the Kongo in the fifteenth century. In other words, Africa has kept faith with African-American soul, in spite of the bitter historic realities of separation upon separation upon separation, black culture in America is an undeniably African culture even, if not especially, in the intimate matters of the heart.

"Bantu" is not an ethnicity but a language group. Bantu culture originated in the Nok region of Nigeria about 2,500 years ago. It then spread over a very large swath of the African continent from Cameroon to Kenya, from the Cape of Good Hope to Uganda. As I say in *The Village of the Water Spirits*, "Likely shaped by ancient Egyptian culture across the Sahel and the Sahara, there are many Bantu languages and many Bantu cultures, and at the same time, they make a fairly coherent whole. They are certainly united around the sacredness of water, and I know of no Bantu culture where water does not play a central role."

The way blacks carried this coherence and the primacy of water to America through the transatlantic slave trade seems now both a mystery and an inevitability.

In *The Myth of the Negro Past*, Melville Herskovits was the first to note, in 1941, that "the primary ritual in black Baptist culture in America, full immersion baptism, was African in origin." Herskovits continues: "The intransigence of the priests of the river cult was so marked that, more than any other group of holy men, they were sold into slavery to rid the conquerors of troublesome leaders. In all parts of the New World where African religious beliefs have persisted, moreover, the river cult or in broader terms, the cult of the water spirits, holds an important place."

The understanding of current scholars is that Bantu culture had an overwhelming influence on what was to become

African-American culture. About forty percent of those sold in the slave ports of the American South were Bantu. Winifred K. Vass, in *The Bantu Speaking Heritage of the United States*, writes: "Bantu speaking slaves from central Africa enjoyed a linguistic unity and ability to communicate with their fellow captives that slaves of West Africa did not share." For the century before and the century after Emancipation, blacks were the majority in Georgia, the Carolinas, Tennessee, and Mississippi.

I write all this in shorthand, the long sweep of history itself always rich with the unknowable. From Egypt, singing to water from oasis to oasis, to Nigeria and south to Central Africa, keeping cattle, working metal, initiating the boys, the girls, and those who were called to medicine. Then the sweep to the multiple cultures that were enslaved, Mandaza's Shona people at the eastern end of the Zambezi Triangle through the diaspora from the Congo and Angola to Charleston, New Orleans, Detroit, St. Louis, and south-central L.A.

By the time of our second initiation, Mandaza and I had entered into the eloquent give-and-take of the dance: initiation through dialogue. For one rite I would be his *nganga*, and for another he'd call on the spirits to initiate me.

"Remember, Michael, human beings cannot initiate other human beings. It is the spirits that do the initiation."

How to truly tell the story of twins born to different mothers, different races, altogether different worlds? How to wade into the mystery of twinship itself, to make clearer what is utterly mysterious? Utterly Mysterious.

Once Mandaza took me to the village of his spirits, deep in the rainforest alongside the Zambezi River. The village was a small grove of trees, a haven of monkeys and centipedes, certainly never a place of human habitation. I sang a song of gratitude for being welcomed; Mandaza left a little sacred snuff as an offering of "food" for the spirits and placed in my palm a pinch to inhale. Feeding the spirits: inner and outer were now apiece. "This is the village where the spirits of the twins were born."

Being a new initiate, I relied on Mandaza's eyes. I could not see the village and so inquired of the Tarot what God was wanting to convey here. The knight of swords imaged as the Dioscuri, Castor and Polydeuces, the warrior twins born to the mortal Leda and the father of the gods, Zeus. Gemini. One being human and the other a god, yet they were inseparable. When Polydeuces died, it was arranged that they would alternate, one day together among the gods of Olympus, the next day in the invisible world of Hades where those who have passed from this life live.

Mandaza received this old Greek story as if it were African: the visible and invisible interfused, twinned and twined.

The Dioscuri are the *midzimu* (or as a Jungian might say, the archetypes) that inform this book. The attentive reader will note the edge between Mandaza's life and mine, the shimmering frontier where we connect and separate. She will note the edges between each of us and the Invisibles, also shimmering. The story is an intimately personal one, but this shimmering is not us. It is the presence of the Dioscuri.

Although Mandaza and I are twinned, it would be silly to impose an artificial symmetry between his story and mine or, more accurately, between his way of telling his story and my very Western memoir. Symmetry is immediately broken by the fact that autobiography is not a traditional African form. It took some effort to get my dear *mapatya,* my twin, to sit still and talk into my minicassette recorder. The fact that Mandaza's story is composed on the tongue while mine is sifted through the various layers of self-consciousness within which the written word thrives illustrates something of the cultural distance across which we recognized our essential twinship.

The Bantu shaman, or *nganga,* is a master of the word, and Mandaza is eloquent and charismatic in both Shona and English. The translucent direct statement is highly valued among Bantu people. One's cards are laid out on the table, nothing hidden. From that translucency a *nganga* like Mandaza evaluates his life in relationship to "the others"—those spirits that have called him to the practice of healing. And so his story proceeds not so much asking "What is inside of me?" but "What is the community of the living and the dead that I am inside of, that I serve?" As his apprentice, I have learned much from the agility with which Mandaza moves between various ethnic worlds—Shona, Ndebele, Bushmen, Tonga, Native American, European, Chinese, Hindu, and the worlds of the living and the dead.

My story is written from a different angle, the heart of the narrative asking "What is inside of me?" and "How is it that this vagrant soul became an African *nganga*?" I am an alumnus of psychoanalysis. The very years when Mandaza was being initiated by an old shaman of the nearby Ndebele tribe, I was writhing on the analytic couch beneath the benevolent gaze of Dr. John Seeley. The shamanic rite that is the heart of true psychoanalysis is a terrible descent by way of storytelling to the true stuff of one's interior life. Such a rite is not African, and becoming a *nganga* has not made me an African man.

One of my pleasures with Mandaza has been the rich exchange between two different ways of knowing, two different ways of telling a story.

All this being said, we are twinned, from the nearly fatal infections we both acquired in our navels when we were babies to the displacements of our childhoods, from our Christian educations and later rejections of Christianity to our political awakenings during times of historical turmoil, from the ferocious ordeals that made us healers to that radiant moment when lives lived apart and parallel suddenly came together on the banks of the Zambezi. It would have been so much easier to write a book about Mandaza's life story or my own, but it seems that those twin brothers in the village of the ancestors who brought the two of us together have their own story to tell. Mandaza's story and my own interweave chapter by chapter so that between the two stories perhaps one story can be heard, a story that belongs to neither him nor me but comes from the spirits we serve.

This book is crafted as a gift to a world divided by race. That is its intent. Mandaza and I know the power of twinship across tribes because we are living it.

I imagine that you join us now at the side of the Zambezi River. As the sun goes down we gather dry elephant dung and driftwood to start a fire to keep the lions away. The green flicker of fireflies delights us, and the roar of Moziyatunya—Victoria Falls—is softened by distance. A long night of telling the twins' story is before us.

Thank you for accompanying us to this sacred place.

MAPATYA

MANDAZA: Before I met Michael I had no twin, no *mapatya*. What happened is that I had a dream when I was being initiated by an Ndebele *nganga*, Mr. Ndlovu. In the dream I was looking for my brother in the Matopos Hills. I was near the caves at Siloswane. I met people who were coming out of the caves, and I asked them if they had seen my twin brother who is a white man. I went from one cave to another inside the mountain looking for this brother of mine.

Some people said they saw him inside the mountain. So I went inside to find him, but before I found him, I woke up. Michael also was having dreams in America that told him how to recognize his twin, a black man. And Simakuhle, my wife, too had seen Michael many times in her dreams before he arrived. She was told, "One of the sons of this family is coming home." That is the way these spirits work. This is the way it is with family.

So when we met a few years later, we recognized each other. It was surprising, but we had been prepared by our spirits. The way Michael was born and grew up was identical to how I was born and grew up. He almost died when he was born, and I also almost died when I was born.

When I look at Michael's life when he was a street kid without a home, I remember that I did not have a home either. I moved from one place to another, being looked after by strangers. At times I would go without food when I was working for these people. Michael also was hungry. So this *mapatya* issue is real, very real.

After I initiated Michael, he in turn initiated me. There was a give-and-take—"Do me service and I do you service." That is the way of twins who are *nganga*s. As twins and *nganga*s we have to do the work together to heal the people together. He is healing people in the United States; I am healing people in Africa. When he comes here, we heal together. This is how our spirits operate.

When I first had a dream about having a twin who was a white man, it was confusing. I thought this was an obstacle in the way of my spirits. Generally speaking, Africans do not know that whites have ancestors and can get trance possessed. So when I saw that Michael had some spirits, that white people also have spirits on them, it was quite a shock to me.

When the missionaries came, they said, "Ancestors are no good. They are evil spirits." But to my surprise I see that lots of white people also have ancestors, and they get trance possessed. And there are also *nganga*s who are white people. Now no one can tell me that whites don't have ancestors because I am initiating them, and I am seeing their spirits. It seems possible to me that there are no human beings without ancestor spirits upon them.

As soon as Michael gets trance possessed, I get trance possessed. We work together in trance possession even when he is in America. If Michael has problems in the United States, I can sense it from this far. I think of him immediately and feel depressed. When we talk on the phone, I find out he is having problems.

Before we met there was a missing element in both of our lives. Michael had to be initiated by my spirits, and I also had to be initiated by his spirits. When we met and initiated one another, for the two of us the initiation was complete and this missing element disappeared. We were then cemented as *mapatya*. We find it difficult to separate. Now I can say we complete each other constantly.

When I look at twinship, I look at the twinship between all ancestors, both black and white ancestors being the children of God. Twinship creates permanent friendship. When I look in the face of my white twin, I know the rule of colonialism and racism is over.

Let us look at the ancestors: the Zulu ancestors, the Shona ancestors, the Bushmen ancestors. They all come with the same message: that we are one people and we all worship one God. They believe and know they were created by God in his image. If the people everywhere followed that principle, there would be peace today. But we have created divisions and multiple groupings that don't see eye to eye at all. We are confining ourselves into holding cells. We are unfree. There are walls around every home. What are we afraid of—our neighbor? There is no twinship there.

Some people go to Israel to pray. Fine. My people go under a big tree. Does it matter where one goes to pray? It is what comes from inside our hearts. My heart, my behavior, is God's temple. If I give myself up to my God, I give myself up to my ancestors totally and openly. In this way I am creating twinship here—one world united by my actions, not by what I say with my mouth.

If my spirits are your spirits, and your spirits are my spirits, there is nothing more to say. What I've learned from this twinship is very broad. The question is: "Mandaza, how do you treat your neighbors be they black or white?" What does Europe do to their neighbor Africa? What does Africa do to their neighbor America? And so forth.

This is the way of Grandmother Spider. This is how she makes a web to support the peacemakers. She says, "To complete a true initiation, one has to be initiated by different people. And the different people must also be initiated by other people as well." Michael was not initiated by one person; he was initiated by many people. With me it was the same. I was not initiated by Michael alone but by many other people as well. I was recently initiated by the Bushmen. They had a dream that I was going to be initiated by them. Simakuhle also had a dream that I was to be initiated by the Bushmen. This is twinship in the broadest sense.

This is the desire of the ancestors. They say, "If you become one family, you will solve many problems." If we create twinship in this way, we would not be creating weapons of war. What for? To kill my neighbor?

We can also make twinship with the earth. We can also make twinship with the animals, with the birds. Look at what we are doing to the earth today. It is a dumping place for our poisons. Some nuclear weapons are hidden in the earth. The water and the air are polluted. No wonder we have so many diseases today. They were not sent by God or our ancestors. We are making those diseases ourselves.

We do not own the land; the land owns us. We do not own the universe; the universe owns us. We do not own God or the ancestors; they own us. It is as simple as that. So we must make twinship between these things.

St. Peter was told by Jesus, "If you want to follow me, leave everything behind you and come after me." That was a particular incident, that one—a particular call from God. For most people the demand is not so great. It is simply a matter of realizing who you are and where you came from.

My way, the same as with Michael and Simakuhle, was like that of St. Peter, and "now, not later," is what God said. I tried to escape but I couldn't, and I was taken deeper and deeper into the circle of God's presence until I had only one response: "Here I am." One response and one responsibility—to heal.

There was no longer an obstacle I could put between me and this experience of "Here I am." Nothing at all. That is when initiation occurs, when there is no other place to go, just this place.

Initiation through different people creates this twinship. The twinship is with God and everything and not just between Michael and Mandaza.

MICHAEL AND MANDAZA'S STORY

The spider's touch, how exquisitely fine!
Feels at each thread and lives along the line.

—Alexander Pope

1

▼ ▼ ▼ ▼ ▼

I JUST THOUGHT IT WAS THE WAY THINGS WERE

MANDAZA: When I started to know about life, I didn't know I had problems in the way I was growing up. I just thought it was the way things were.

This story I heard from my mother: When my umbilical cord was cut, I became very ill. A trance medium came through the village, and the spirit said through her, "Take this child out of the village and make him a shelter in the bush. Don't give him any medication. Just take him into the bush and sit quietly with him, and he will heal."

So they took me into the bush and made a little shelter from branches. My mother nursed me in this little shelter for three weeks. She was the only one allowed to be there with me. When we returned to the village together, I was healed.

I first heard this story two years ago when my wife, Simakuhle, was asking my mother about my life. She wanted to know why I was always sick. Sometimes I'm well. The next few days I'm in bed, and I'm not feeling well at all. You know, the spirits come heavily on me at times. Very heavily indeed. I feel like I want to sleep all the time. I don't like to eat anything at all. That worries Simakuhle a lot. She knows a little bit about my life from our marriage. But my mother knows me since my birth.

My mother also told me about my father's death. He died at the hands of witches when I was young, so I don't remember him at all.

He was working in Bulawayo, my father, when I was born. He had a job building a round house, and some neighbors invited him to have some beer. But in the beer there were some dangerous herbs, and he started complaining of stomach problems, and he swelled up like a watermelon.

These witches took the cup away from him and got rid of it before anyone could know.

Some people went to report this to the police in Chivo town. There were no buses back then so someone had to go by bicycle, but when the police came, my father had already died. His whole body was swollen and he was black like charcoal. A postmortem was carried out. He was destroyed inside. His intestines were in pieces.

That is how my father died. Why did they kill him? I don't know. But in that particular community almost no one was working, and he was. Perhaps that is why they killed him.

When I was maybe five years old, I liked to make things with wood and stone. One day I took an axe and was working on a piece of wood and cut myself on my finger. I was bleeding profoundly.

My mother was in Harare looking for some work so she could support my brother and myself. So it was left to my grandmother to carry me to the hospital about fifty kilometers from where we lived—on her back! The nurses who were there told her to dress the wound herself. This is the way they were trained—no kindness, no mercy. "You have come to us with your sick child. That's your problem. You dress the wound. You wash it." As old as she was, there was no respect for her.

She would take me twice a week, and then she was tired so it would be only once a week. And the wounded finger was getting worse. I was told she decided to use the herbs from the bush to heal this wound because I was at the point of death. With the herbs the wound healed finally.

During those very, very early years, I hated *ngangas*. I didn't want to be near them. I thought they were witches. They would frighten me. I just didn't go along with them at all. When they were dancing to appease the spirits, I would say, "Get out of the place!" As young as I was, I used to think there must be one God who looks after all. So why the dances, this trance possession, which looks very frightening?

When people would take snuff, *bute,* I would not want to sit next to them. These healing ceremonies meant nothing to me at all, and yet I loved to help the wounded and the sick.

I was a boy who grew up afraid to see people fighting, to see any form of violence. I would try to say, "Why can't you stop immediately?" I remember one time when I was in very early school and children came around me, trying to make me fight with another person. I'd just look at them and start crying. I remember this well. And one time I went to primer school outside Harare, and the bigger boys came around me, saying, "You're an excellent athlete. You run so well. But why do you do it? Why do you do it around here? We're going to beat you tomorrow. When you're in the field, we're going to get you."

Not long after that, they started pushing me around. This bigger boy came with the other boys, and he slapped me on the face. What came over me that time I don't know, because I just found him lying on the floor, and I was in tears. I was shivering and shaking, and somebody said, "You hit him." Well, I was just in tears. I wasn't happy really to see a violent situation.

That's the way these ancestor spirits work, you see. They wanted me to be a healer and a peacemaker even when I was a child, but I didn't know that yet. Becoming a *nganga* for me was a long, hard path.

2

■ ■ ■ ■ ■

OF SUCH SMALL THINGS
THE KINGDOM OF HEAVEN
IS MADE

MICHAEL: Ah, yes, my story. How I became a *nganga*. How I found my twin. In fact, the story begins before my birth.

Shortly before I went to Africa to be initiated, I consulted an astrologer in Los Angeles, a fellow named Leor. In Zimbabwe he would be called a *nganga*. I asked him under what sign was the dark of the moon before my parents made love to conceive me. I wanted to find the pathway to the realm of the ancestors, and for some reason I thought this information might help me.

The dark of the moon before my conception fell close to the summer solstice, the brightest day of the year. However, there was a full eclipse of the sun. So the moon was dark that night, and the sun was black during the day, both under the sign of the warrior twins. "I don't know what this means," he said, "except that you are going to Africa to meet your twin brother."

The night I was conceived the moon was nearly full, or so my mother tells me. I like beginning my story like this. I feel a happiness when I think of my parents enjoying one another and a freedom in remembering that once I did not exist. I am reminded that Jesus said the Kingdom of Heaven is like a tiny mustard seed. The moment of my parent's pleasure, the planting of the seed, the gift of this life from its beginning to its end—of such small things, Jesus would say, the Kingdom of Heaven is made.

I was born in the spring of 1957, the first of four brothers with two older sisters. After I was born, like Mandaza, I was very, very sick. I got a staph infection in my navel, and I was hospitalized because of it. To cure me they gave me a drug to which I turned out to be extremely allergic. My mother had a priest come to say the last rites for me because they didn't think I would live.

The infection in my navel and the horror of the suffering of how I came into the world put a kind of terror and rage and hunger in my body that I've lived with most of my life—lived with, in fact, until I was initiated by Mandaza. As a child, I would have nightmares, remembering being a baby. When I was seven years old, I would put a knife to my gut and dare myself to stick it in. When I became a teenager, sexual feelings were especially terrifying. Often it seemed as if having a body was itself unbearable.

This was in the American Southwest, in New Mexico, where both my parents are from, my father a white, my mother a Mexican. My mother's people are brown-skinned, a mixed breed of Native American and the Spanish who conquered that part of the world about four hundred years ago. However, when it comes to skin color I am certainly a white man.

From the time I was a child my race has not made a whole lot of sense to me. My father's family was racist. It is rumored his mother remarried a member of the Ku Klux Klan, which hates black people, Mexicans, and others. I grew up with little connection to my white family.

When I was growing up, my race would change twice a day. At home, I was Mexican, but when I was out on the street, the *pachucos,* the Mexican gang kids, beat me up for being white. In New Mexico when you're a half-breed, you're called "coyote"—the wild dog that they say changes shape wherever he goes.

The funny thing is, now that I have an African family, I continue to change shape everywhere I go. In Zimbabwe, because I'm a mixed breed, legally I'm called "colored." When I walk down the street, I am white. When I am with my African family, I'm Shona and Ndebele. And when I work as a *nganga,* I usually sing in the Yoruba language, or in Navajo or Spanish or Hebrew or Japanese or whatever little bits of other languages I know how to pray in. All of my life I've changed shapes. That's what my life has been about.

3

▼▼▼▼▼

CURLED UP
LIKE A CHICKEN FOOT

MANDAZA: One time—I think I was probably under ten
years of age—my uncle was hit by a lightning bolt, and his
hand was curled up like a chicken foot. My elder aunt was
there with her daughter, crying, looking at my uncle. He was
lying there, and they couldn't do anything. So I went into the
bush and brought some fiber from a tree and tied it with a
stick like a splint, opening his hand and fingers, tying the
stick up to his elbow. After two days his hand healed. He was
able to spread his fingers. That was my first experience as a
healer. Since you have asked me to tell my story, I can now
remember this, but at that time it probably meant nothing to
me. My uncle was also a healer. Though I didn't like *nganga*s,
my uncle was different. I trusted him.

I am told that when I was very young he did some work
on me. I have cuts on my body that he made. My family
showed them to me when I was grown up. Why the spirits in
him did it, he didn't know—but he was told by the spirits to do
it for me. So the first initiation done in my lifetime was done
by my uncle.

Now that my uncle is dead, he is the one who comes to me
whenever I am in trouble, and he says, "We are with you. Why
should you worry?" I see him clearly in my visions. He talks
to me.

When he was still living, he had personal problems with
me at times, but truly speaking, he loved me so much. He

treated me like his own brother. We played games like little kids. He'd chase me around in the home. And whatever food was served to him, he would not eat it alone but would call me to him so we would eat together.

When somebody dies when they are young, I see them change and mature in my dreams. It seems there is a purification that takes place when they are dead. There is a difference between how they behaved when they were living and how they approach you now that they are dead.

As a spirit, my uncle fully understands me—what I am and what I'm carrying. That is why he comes in a mature way, a supportive way, to show me the path. As a spirit he is wise and mature and gives me wisdom.

4

■ ■ ■ ■ ■

THE STRANGER
GOD GAVE ME TO LOVE

MICHAEL: My mother is Catholic, and my father was a Buddhist. He grew up in a strict and oppressive Southern Baptist family. When he was thirteen years old, he saw an advertisement in a comic book about the Theosophists and the Mysteries of the East. So he wrote away for their material, and he became Alamogordo, New Mexico's first Buddhist—first and only, I think.

So I was raised between two spiritual traditions. During my first years I practiced Catholicism, then I started practicing Buddhism. For a while I practiced both.

However, for about eight months when I was fourteen, I became a born-again Christian, a Pentecostal. We were living near Detroit, where my mother was going to the university. I couldn't stand sharing a room with my brother Martin, so I made the closet under the stairs my bedroom. Jack Kerouac had nothing on my cool pad. My Beatles poster, my copy of Chairman Mao's little red book, and late nights with Brother Bogel, a ghetto preacher and healer shouting through the radio into my stoned hippie brain.

Folks would call in to his program. Terribly sick people or someone with a mad daughter or a father who was a stone-cold drunk. "I rebuke thee, Satan, in the name of Jee-sus!" Brother Bogel would shout, and after his healing he'd call those who hadn't accepted Christ to kneel before the radio and pray, repenting their sins and receiving Christ as Lord and Savior. I did so. I most certainly didn't want to go to hell, and it was obvious the world was soon going to end.

For my first three months, I was a "closeted" Christian, not because I didn't preach to friends at school and strangers on the street (mostly about the apocalypse), but because I had no community at all. Or rather, my church was Brother Bogel and the black folk I heard on the radio.

I knew this wouldn't do, so I hitchhiked to Ann Arbor to seek flesh-and-blood Christians. God does indeed work in mysterious ways. Within five minutes of arriving, I got a ride with Reverend Bill Brown, who was off to a Pentacostal meeting: the Word of God community. Several hundred people singing ecstatically in tongues and prophesying and laying on hands. Soon I was "baptized in fire" and was speaking in tongues myself. Nothing prepared me for being a *nganga* quite like this immersion as a young boy.

But strangely, I was never baptized in water—except as a very Catholic baby.

I was walking past a black church in Ann Arbor one day, and it was full of singing and clapping, so I shyly went in and was greeted with enthusiasm. They were baptizing a girl in a white dress, a schoolmate of mine. She was radiant. For a long time after that, even after I stopped being a Christian, every fiber of me longed to be baptized. But there was something else in me, very stubborn, that refused. I sensed that I really didn't know what life was about and somehow understood that such a commitment to Christianity would keep me from finding out.

Something happened when I was a Pentecostal, however, that completely changed my life. Mandaza's story about tending to his uncle when he was struck by lightning reminds me of it.

I was adopted as something of a spiritual son by Reverend Bill, and one day he gave me a Bible and asked me to go witness to a fellow named George who was living in a cheap hotel. Fresh from the gutter, George was a drunk who was drying out and trying to put his life into order.

While I was reading scripture to George, he toppled over and started convulsing on the floor, shaking his head and slobbering. I had never seen an epileptic seizure before and don't think I even knew what one was. I ran off in a panic to get a couple of friends who lived nearby to help me with this situation. But they weren't at home.

When I returned to George's room, he was gone. I searched the neighborhood and soon spied him walking along a busy street a couple of blocks away. As I caught up with and walked alongside him it quickly became clear that he didn't know who I was or where he was going. All he remembered was that his name was George and that he had once been in the Navy. I persuaded him to return with me to the hotel.

Over the next two or three hours I was able to encourage his memory and then his personality to come forth, bit by bit. After a while he even remembered who I was. What I recall most from that day was the luminosity of the light of late afternoon and the easy tenderness I felt toward this stranger whom God had given me to love.

That evening I went to a prayer meeting and told my story, and the circle prayed over me. A woman was taken by the Holy Spirit—in Africa they would say she was trance possessed—and prophesied that the gift of healing had come upon me, that I was to be a healer.

That prayer meeting was the beginning of the end of my life as a Christian. For years afterward I thought I was the butt of one of God's jokes. I had been given the gift of healing, I thought, but I wouldn't step forward with it. I remember looking at a blind man across the aisle from me in a city bus and feeling tormented, knowing that if I truly had faith, I could and would lay hands on him and he would see. Everywhere I went, I saw people around me afflicted in one way or another, and each became a living testimony to my lack of faith, to how endlessly afraid I was.

In retrospect, of course, I'm not so unkind with myself. It seems that the spirit of the gift is always looking for an open window, and my meeting with George presented just such an opportunity. It was then that I stepped onto the path of healing. A fourteen-year-old can be forgiven for not having a clue about the consequences or meaning of being a vessel for such a spirit.

5

▼▼▼▼▼

THE LION TOTEM

MANDAZA: All tribes have totems. I've discovered this is even true of white people. We have the *mvumbwe* totem, which is the Zimbabwe bird totem. We have the zebra totem. We have the buffalo totem. We've got the cow totem, the fish totem. My family totem, for all the generations through the father line, is *shumba*–lion. A little *shumba* was born in me. When I get trance possessed, I see the lion roaring in me, and I behave like a lion.

We identify ourselves by our totem. Different people are scattered all over Africa. But when they say, "I am a *shumba*," I know they are my relative. When we meet a stranger, one of the first things we ask is, "What totem are you?" When a number of us lions are together, everything softens up, and we are one family immediately.

The spirits that are upon me are also one family because they are allowed to be on me by the lion. The *shumba* invites them and welcomes them. No other spirits can come through our family without the permission of the *shumba* ancestors.

The lion is at the beginning of my people, and through *shumba* we connect to other tribes and people of different races. My ancestors can welcome anybody because there is nothing above the lion. The first man of my tribe assumed the lion totem; I don't know how exactly the idea of having totems among people originated, but I understand my people chose the lion as the totem. Yet I am trance possessed by other animal spirits as well: the white eagle and the spider woman, for example.

———

CHAPTER 5

Our ancestors worshipped God, whom we call Mwari. They did not have churches or temples. They used to go to particular trees like the *chikata* tree, which is a fruit tree. Different groups of people would go to different trees. Our ancestors believed that God lives everywhere, so some went under these trees to worship. When they offered their prayers for rain, the rain would come.

Our ancestors knew they were created by Mwari so they worshipped him. We ask our ancestors to take our prayers to Mwari because they are so close to him. That link cannot be broken because Mwari gives us everything we have.

When the Bible says "Honor your parents," it does not say the living parents or the dead parents. It just says honor your mother and father. We also go to the grave sites of our ancestors. We know there is a soul in that grave.

When God created things, he said, "Let me create man and woman in my image." Those are our ancestors, and their ancestor was God; so there is a direct link all the way back to the beginning. It is critical for us to keep this chain unbroken so that we are without obstacles between us and God. God's law is very clear: honor your parents and honor me. This is also the way someone like me returns through Christianity back to the way of the ancestors—through the parents. Even now I believe Adam was my ancestor, Abraham was my ancestor, Eve was my ancestor.

6

■ ■ ■ ■ ■

THE LANGUAGE
OF THE BIRDS

MICHAEL: When I was a little boy, I loved God so much. Some boys want to grow up and be cowboys or astronauts. I wanted to grow up to be St. Francis of Assisi. I was very close to animals, especially the birds and the insects. My best friend, Tad Brown, and I started a bird-watching society when I was ten years old. We decided that when we got out of high school we would get a sailboat and sail to the Indian Ocean to see if the dodo bird was really extinct. All we cared about was birds. The other kids called us "the bird brains."

Everybody at school knew I was interested in birds, and one day a girl I thought was pretty told me there was an owl in her backyard. After school we walked up and down the alleyway behind her house looking for the owl, but with no luck. Just then, I heard the screech of a blue jay and recognized it as the bird's distress call. I knew the owl was farther up the alleyway and the blue jay was screaming at it. I suggested that the pretty girl and I walk on, and sure enough, I was right—there was the owl in a walnut tree. I was so proud that I could understand the language of the birds. That was one of the best moments of my childhood.

My parents divorced when I was eleven. For a few years after that my mother, my three brothers, and I would move every year. My mother was trying to get an education so she could support us. By the time I dropped out of high school, I had gone to eight different schools.

CHAPTER 6

We were poor, and for a couple of years we lived in my grandparents' basement. I left my white childhood behind and moved in with my Mexican family, and all the rules changed. For a white boy a child's life is about playing. In my Mexican childhood we worked on my grandfather's ranch, which had apple, apricot, and peach trees; maize fields and wild chokecherry, spinach, mint, and raspberries growing alongside the Rio Pacheco; goats and chickens and an immense white horse to plow the fields.

We worked all the time. On the one hand, I loved working on the ranch; on the other, I hated it because I felt my childhood was being stolen from me. I felt seen not with affection but as a worker, another pair of hands to work the fields. It took me probably twenty years not to feel bitter about that— twenty years to forgive my grandfather.

After my parents' divorce, my father started drinking beer and liquor, and eventually he drank himself to death. It took him eight years to do it. It was hard for him to be divorced, and he felt such sadness for the world that all he could do was drink. He was fifty-two years old when he died.

During those eight years I lived away from him most of the time, yet we became very close. When I was fifteen, he taught me how to do Buddhist meditation. He was my first spiritual teacher. I soaked in his wisdom as I watched him kill himself. I cried about his death for years. I had just begun to know him when he died.

7

▼▼▼▼▼

WORDS TO TALK
ABOUT GOD

MANDAZA: So many people cared for me—different people, different homes altogether—not because they really loved me but because, as human beings, they couldn't throw me out of their village. Somehow these people had to look after me because I was almost like an orphan at that time. Year after year it was this or that relative saying, "I want that child here," and this or that parent saying, "I want that child there." Whoever had some work to be done would say, "I want that boy for a year."

From year to year to year, I was looking for some form of education. I was wandering from this village to the next village. I was very motivated. I don't know where this came from, but I just loved being educated. Unfortunately, I couldn't get the best education I wanted. I would hardly spend two years at one school. The type of instruction I got was very poor, from those who were willing to offer their services for free to a person such as I was.

I was always on the move. Luckily, at whatever school I attended I would find someone who was willing to take me in for a year. I even went to the little African farm schools where I could offer my services working the fields. They, in turn, would look after me and give me food and a home to stay in. I do not know how old I was. I could have been nine or ten years old, because I knew what I was doing the way a very young child does not.

The British government, when it was in power in this country, set the standards for education. First there was Substandard A for every child starting school. Usually one goes into Substandard A at age seven, but some started school older than that, especially in the rural schools during the colonial era. Then you went on to Substandard B, then Standard 3, Standard 4, and so on up to Standard 6. After that you started Form 1 and continued to Form 6 and then to university. For me it was almost impossible to get to Standard 6 level. But I wanted to go further with my education. I wanted so much to go even to the university.

By our custom my father's brother should have looked out for me through my life. He would have been my second father. Once when I was visiting my mother near Harare, I met my uncle. He was a businessman with a fleet of lorries. He said he was going to care for me.

What I wanted was to go to school, but when he saw me, he thought to himself, "Oh, yes. I have got another man who can work here for me." I worked for him, yes, but when he saw I wasn't interested in business at all, he helped me find my way to Highfield Community School.

Highfield was formed by the Nationalists. Robert Mugabe, the first president of this country, was very much involved in the opening of this school. The Nationalists had seen the terrible plight young people were in because of the oppression of the Africans by the whites who ruled the country at that time. The whites really tried not to build more schools for Africans. What they wanted was cheap labor on their farms, in their factories, and so forth. That was the situation.

At that time the Nationalist parties, ZANU and ZAPU, were legal, but the children of the Nationalists were not allowed in the government schools because the whites thought they would influence the other children. So the Nationalists decided to form community schools. The government allowed it because they believed we would for sure get a poor education and go nowhere at all. But the Nationalists hired teachers from outside of the country. We even had British teachers, American teachers—white people, for that matter.

Highfield was a legal institution under apartheid, but it was in a difficult situation. The politicians had been fighting for the school. Most of the teachers were Nationalists themselves. There were oh so many children, boys and girls. I remember there were seven classes of Form 1 that were operating under the trees. Groups of children under that tree here and under that tree over there and under that tree with the teachers writing on slabs. It was difficult, but we enjoyed it because we were getting what we wanted.

When I completed my Form 2, I applied to some neighboring countries to get a better education and got accepted at a school in Uganda. But the government would not allow the students from Highfield to get placed anywhere outside this country. When the government became aware that there were some very intelligent young men and girls coming from Highfield Community School, they decided to seal us off. Soldiers were ordered to surround the whole school, and they placed tattoos on our forearms to make sure that wherever we went we were recognized. We couldn't go to Harare, couldn't go outside this country—in fact, we couldn't go outside Highfield. We had to stay in Highfield under very high security and couldn't leave for any reason. Wherever we went under apartheid, we had to produce identification cards. But if we were from Highfield, we'd have to show our forearm, and we'd be asked, "Why are you here at this place? You are supposed to be at Highfield." Then they would pick us up, put us in a big truck, and send us back.

Highfield students were not allowed any education after Form 6. We were not allowed to go to any college outside Harare, so I had to sneak into colleges outside the capital. Around that time I got an opportunity to take a course on teaching children at a college in the Mutoko area. I went there with friends, but we had to be careful because the police were looking for us. Fortunately, the principal of this college was a Nationalist himself. He understood our plight. "Whatever comes," he said, "I am ready for it."

At this school I was very much involved in Boy Scouting. We trained the boys to rely upon themselves when they were in the bush and to look after the old people in local homes. These were my services to the people. I was also involved in theater, where I acted as Joseph at the birth of Jesus. Later I acted as Pilate at the Crucifixion. We produced two records from those two dramas, and they sold well in this country.

Still, I wasn't inspired by the education I was getting. I wanted to go even further, but getting the fee to go to this particular school was difficult. Money for uniforms! During vacations I continued working at the college for certain teachers so I could get money.

I was learning to teach children, and, in my second year, I was chosen head boy of the whole college by the staff. I was beginning to gain a reputation of being quite good at teaching the little ones.

After completing a year as a student teacher, I was transferred to another school to teach. The following year I was transferred to another school and yet another. They were saying, "You have got the ability to develop schools. You can develop a very poor school into a better school, so we'd rather change you from one school to another. We want your ideas to be shared." If education at a school was poor, I'd ask: How could we better it? How could we make use of extra time to be with the schoolchildren and give them more education? Why couldn't we have afternoon sessions to continue teaching these children? Why couldn't we offer them more visual aids so they could see how things develop naturally? Sometimes I'd look at the way staff meetings were handled by the headmaster and see that he was dictating to the teachers what to do. I'd say: Why can't we share ideas? Then we'd make use of everyone's ideas and come up with a sound education. This is what my spirits led me to do and say.

Because I'm talking about my education, I should talk about Christianity. I am not a Christian, but it was the churches that gave me words to talk about God.

The schools I went to practiced Christianity. The first school I went to, when I was perhaps seven years old, was a British Methodist Church school, but I didn't go to church. Church at that time meant nothing to me at all. I didn't know the difference between being a member of the church and not being a member of the church. It was all the same. It was just a matter of playing games with other children while the old people were at their church service.

Later it was the Anglicans who taught us what it meant to be baptized, what it meant to repent, and so forth. If you are not baptized, you are an evil person—this is what they would say to young boys and girls.

I remember very well when they tried to baptize me in the Anglican Church. I was at a mission school in the Chivu area.

At this particular mission we would cook our own food and get our own water from the river. So the young boys and girls went into the woods to collect some firewood to prepare the food before this particular day of baptism.

I was told that someone had seen me walking with a girl collecting firewood. I said, "Yes. That is very true. We were collecting some firewood." I was told that they didn't want me to walk with the opposite sex. Walking with the opposite sex meant nothing to me. It was no different than walking with a boy. They said it was in one of the Commandments. I said, "Well, maybe I don't know about this Commandment. My intention was to gather firewood, that is all."

They said, "You cannot be baptized now." It was a big issue.

Some of my teachers came to intervene, saying, "This young man could not have done anything like that. This is a lie. Somebody must have created a lie here because we know him."

After that they decided I could be baptized, and the headmaster came to me and said, "I see in my vision that I must give you a name, but I cannot tell you it until the day of your baptism."

When I went into the water, the headmaster was at my side, and the priest asked, "What is his name now?" And my teacher said, "I want him to be called Augustine." That's how I got that name. Before that I was called Alexander.

Michael met me as Augustine, and throughout my life since that baptism I've been Augustine. This is the way of colonialism the world over—to rename the natives as European names. But now I am simply Mandaza, the name from long before my baptism, truer to who I am as an African man.

When I began my secondary education, I went to an American Methodist Church Mission School where I was taught by American missionaries. I knew if I did not follow what the missionaries wanted, they might try to find out more about my background. If they found that I had been taught by Nationalists, they would chase me away from their school. I had to be careful.

It was here that I came to love church, especially when they talked about God the creator, how we could serve him. I immediately began teaching Sunday school. We were given bicycles to cycle to local villages to entertain the young little boys and girls. I loved to do that! Ah, I enjoyed that work very much! Even during the cold season, I would say, "I want to go and meet those boys and girls!" Right out there in the local bush, in the surrounding farms.

I began to sense that there is a creator above all, God Almighty. I'd look at the preachers and try to understand whether they knew what they were talking about. I began to see in my inner head that some of these preachers really were preaching so they would be respected by the local people and that they didn't really know much about God. Still, I was convinced that God was there. I stayed even though I did not believe in those religions—Methodist, Anglican, what-what, and so forth. I believed in the God that they were praying to but not the religions themselves. This is my relation to church.

8

■ ■ ■ ■ ■

THE BEGGAR
AT THE CROSSROADS

MICHAEL: The turning point in my life that eventually brought me to Africa happened when I was thirteen. I was gathering purple flowers not far from our house. An old Mexican woman told me they were good for stomachaches. Then I saw a black hobo walking up the railroad tracks. Where they crossed a road, he saw me and walked over. He shook my hand and said, "Could you feed me? I haven't eaten since yesterday. I'd be much obliged if you gave me some food."

This was a part of the United States where you rarely saw black people—lots of Native Americans and Mexicans, but really no blacks. I think my little brothers were frightened. They didn't know what to make of this stranger I brought home. I boiled two hot dogs and made a hot dog and ketchup sandwich. This was my feast for the beggar.

First he prayed for about five minutes. He blessed the food, he blessed me, he blessed my path in life. Only then did he eat. As he left I gave him little candy bars called "Space Food Sticks." The package said the astronauts took them to the moon so they would have enough protein. Then he walked off into the desert. He was going from Kentucky to California to live with his family—all the way across the country.

This man changed my life. Completely. Twenty years later I was to meet him again though in rather a different fashion. When I was studying the Yoruba religion, a West African tradition from Nigeria, I came to understand that this was the spirit they call Eshu Elegba. He's the spirit of the crossroads, and he opens the gates to the Mysteries. When you treat a beggar kindly, miracles can happen.

For five years I did nothing but hitchhike all over the United States, Canada, Mexico, and Guatemala—or else I would jump freight trains and ride with the vegetables. When I was sixteen, I hitchhiked from Southern California to Alaska. The last twelve hundred miles was a gravel road. In Anchorage, I found a mission that gave food to down-and-out Eskimos. I had breakfast with them, and then I hitchhiked across Canada to Newfoundland, which is as far east as you can go in North America.

When I wasn't hitchhiking, I lived on the street. I was homeless for three years, between the ages of seventeen and twenty, in a small town in California. There were basically two things that led me to choose homelessness—though nowadays when somebody asks me about it I usually say, "Well, you have to get an education somehow, don't you?"

One thing that sent me to the street was the president, Richard Nixon. America was at war in Vietnam. I was involved with Catholics who were against the war. It was the Christmas of 1972, and Nixon decided to bomb Vietnam into the Stone Age. It was the Christmas season, when you hear carols about peace in the world everywhere, and the president had decided to bomb the Vietnamese people viciously.

At that point I said, "This is not my country. I love the people; I love the land. But this is not my country anymore." I chose homelessness as a kind of internal exile.

Roughly sixty to seventy Vietnamese died for every American who shed blood in Southeast Asia. But that doesn't really say it. The Americans were combatants. Nine out of ten Vietnamese who died were civilian, altogether one-sixteenth of the population. It was far worse in Cambodia and Laos. The war took the lives of no less than a quarter of the people, again almost all civilians. Given that we participated in the deaths of twenty percent of the population of Cambodia, how much outrage can we have that the Khmer Rouge killed another third in their bizarre autogenocide? After all, we, alongside China and Thailand, armed them; they were our allies in the war of attrition against Vietnam after the fall of Saigon.

Another reason I went to the street was that I wanted to be like the beggar-saint, St. Francis. The funny thing, of course, is that the street quickly corrupts you. I became skilled at stealing food. I rarely begged. It was too humiliating. There was plenty of food in garbage cans, and I was very good at collecting wild food growing in the hills.

It's hard to convey what being on the street is like. I'll tell two stories about it.

I was walking down the street hungry one night, and I came to a bar that was playing music. People were waiting in line in front of the bar to buy tickets. Somebody had spilled a whole bunch of pistachio nuts. I love pistachios. I asked myself, "Do I have the courage to get down in front of these people and pick up these pistachios so I can eat?" I prayed about it and then got on my knees, pretending as if nobody existed but me, and pocketed the nuts. I walked on, but at first I felt so nauseous I couldn't eat them.

Another time when I was hungry I had a great idea about how to get food. In this town by the ocean there was a pier where fishermen would sell fish. I figured that at the end of the day if they thought the fish was too old, they would throw it away. So in the late afternoon I approached an Italian fisherman and asked if he had some old fish I could feed my cat. He was delighted. He said he had three cats of his own, and he asked me all about my cat. I didn't know anything about cats, so I started making up stories. While I was telling him about my cat, he swept fish guts off the floor of his stall and gave me a big plastic bag full of them. "They love this stuff," he said. I thanked him and took my fish guts with me, feeling happy and ridiculous.

While living on the street I spent most of my time in the university library. I had dropped out of school, but I was hungry for knowledge. My days were made up of scavenging for food, spending time with friends, and going to the university to study anything I wanted—poetry, world cultures, plants, philosophy, psychology. I was so interested in all of it, I just soaked it up. I knew I was preparing myself for my life. The truth is, I was preparing myself to be a *nganga,* because all I wanted to do was heal the world. One way or another, all my studies revolved around this desire.

The second year I was on the street, I lost my mind. My life was so painful, and I could hear the spirits calling for me. I think I went crazy because I needed to be with them. In fact, that's what happened. I met an ancestor, an old man who wears animal skins. He was one of the many spirits who kept me company then. Being crazy was not hard, though I was sometimes frightened. I telephoned my father and said, "I'm out of my mind. I'm seeing spirits everywhere."

"It's okay," he replied, "When I was your age, I went through the same thing. It's a rite of passage. You can trust it." Those were the kindest words anybody had ever spoken to me. After that, I knew I could trust the spirits. I was no longer afraid of them.

After I went crazy, life became difficult. The spirits had come, and then they abandoned me. I was left in the dust. For fifteen years, I think, it was as if I was eating ashes every day for breakfast, lunch, and dinner. Some good things went on, but I tasted ash in my mouth all the time.

I moved to San Francisco in 1975. There the garbage cans held no food. I had nothing to eat. I had dysentery for months and would wake up every morning soaked in diarrhea.

I tried to prostitute myself, but I had parasites under my skin and was always scratching. I had open sores on my body, and no one wanted to have sex with me. I suppose there's some bleak humor here. I had gone to the Gates of Hell so I could sell myself as meat at a reasonable price. And those in Hell, who are always hungry, turned me down because the meat was spoiled. As it turned out, this was the time when AIDS was percolating in the city. Those little bugs under my skin saved my life. I've always been grateful to them for that.

When you're homeless, you know you are an object of disgust. You sense you are an object of fear, and everybody's eyes pierce through you—people who pity you, people who want to help you, people who hate you. You're dealing with it all the time. You feel naked. You feel like you have no skin.

When I was at the very bottom, all dust and rags, a couple of times a week I would pass a woman on the street who worked in a local bookshop. She would smile at me and say, "Good morning," as if I were a human. That was the beginning, the middle, and the end of the story.

I knew better than to pursue even a friendship with this woman. I didn't want to frighten her. But that smile, that "Good morning," was the single thread that kept me from falling into the abyss for the last year I was homeless.

Twenty years later, I did a public reading of my first book in her bookstore, and I thanked her. I thought she wouldn't remember this casual act of kindness, though I had thought about it almost every day. But she did remember me. "There was a light you carried," she said. A light? Dear God, I felt damn near extinguished but she saw a light?

Through this story I came to believe that no act of kindness is insignificant. There is no telling its value to the other person or what might come of it.

All this time I felt called to go to spend a year alone in the forest. It was then I was healed by the water spirits, though I didn't know them by name. I went to the coast of Big Sur and off into the woods. I carried in food, books to write in, books to read, candles—everything I needed for a whole year, though I actually only lasted one month. During that month I prayed and tried to understand how I had come into such misery. Every day I would go into the river and say, "Wash away this history. Forgive me. Bring me back to myself." I began to see my ordeal as a pilgrimage to the essential stories that would live in my bones the rest of my life. In this life one suffers a lot for the stories that teach one how to live. Homelessness was the education of a young man's soul. This time alone was the first time I saw myself as an old man. I was only nineteen, and I was shocked that a boy could have an old man's spirit in him. The old man seemed to understand the sad and true meaning of my homelessness. The old man told me that the soul is made up of such stories, but when I asked, "What is this thing you call soul?" he didn't answer. It occurred to me then for the first time that, being as young as I was, I was not yet ready to understand the meaning of my life.

9

WAR

MANDAZA: Remember, all of this—my education, my baptism—was happening during a time of war when we were trying to free the country from colonial rule. In the early sixties the youth were active politically, especially in Harare and Highfield. I was one of the organizers in the Nationalist movement, which was involved with mobilizing the youth so we could force some whites to recognize to some extent that an African was a human being.

At that time a young white man of my age would say, "You say boss to me," just because he was white. When I worked for my uncle, I would take trucks to go and buy firewood from farms owned by whites. The attitude I saw on these white faces! We would be told: "Don't touch that gate there, you black man. Wait for me to say whether you can come in or not." Or the white person would never care to talk to you, but he would tell his gardener, a black person, to come and say, "What do you want?" We'd speak to this white man through his gardener or through his cook.

The Nationalists were saying during that time, "We think that we've talked to the white people for a long, long time, and they don't want to listen." I can remember one Nationalist saying, "It's time to collect stones and throw them. This is the only language white people understand."

There were many demonstrations in support of the Nationalists who were being arrested, but we were told that if we took part in any demonstration, we would be shot. We were told to keep quiet and shut up. If we reacted, they would shoot right away.

I saw this with my own eyes in Highfield. Seven blacks were shot dead while I was looking. Just like that. One by one. The next one. . . . The next one. . . . They were covered in red blankets. In front of me! In a school yard, you know, on open ground. One by one. And oh, yes, with children around and parents. Shot dead in my own Highfield. I won't forget that one. It is still there in my mind.

I saw one man who was shot in the leg. The leg was in pieces. My uncle was there sitting with me. I stood up and went straight to this man to help him. I dragged him into our yard, and my uncle said, "The police are going to kill us."

I said, "It's better that they kill every one of us." I won't forget this.

I tied the leg to support it and stopped a taxi. It was illegal for anyone to stop a taxi to carry someone who was injured in this war, but I did, and I dragged the man into the taxi and said, "Please, driver, take this man to the hospital right now." And he did, for free.

My uncle was rather dissatisfied with what I was doing. He was not happy at all. I was going to get us into deep problems with the police and the government. But nothing bad happened at all in our home, even though I was involved in a rather secret something that was going on.

You know, the only weapons we could use in Highfield were stones. What else could we use? But the whites had every weapon at their disposal, not to shoot animals but to shoot blacks. And we used road blocks. This was the 1960s, the 70s, and so forth, before independence in 1980. We would set road blocks along major roads. If the police were going to detain the Nationalists, why not detain the police? All the roads in Highfield, all the roads in Harare blocked with barricades and so forth, drums, broken bottles—putting them on the road so we could protect the Nationalists. We knew that if these leaders were taken away from us, we would be helpless. We went on a rampage and destroyed the street lights so the police could not identify the homes of the Nationalists. But I was more interested in helping the injured during the operations. I liked doing it. That was my major task, really. I wanted to take care of the suffering people.

Every family in the country was touched by the insurrection. Even now, as a *nganga* I tend to the spirits that were wounded during those years. Even my own mother. I remember during this liberation war my mother came to see me. She was living in the Mangaron area near Mozambique. I advised my mother not to go back home during that day or the following day. I felt in my heart that something bad would happen, but she insisted.

She went by way of open truck because buses were not operating in those areas where the war was very hot. The truck hit a land mine and killed almost everybody, including the driver. My mother was thrown some meters away from the explosion, and her legs were broken. I was told that security forces carried her by helicopter to Harare Hospital. The security forces came across this piece of paper with my name on it and phoned the school where I was working so I would know what had happened. That is how I was informed.

10

■ ■ ■ ■ ■

THE BLACK
LIBERATION ARMY

MICHAEL: After I returned from Big Sur, I was just as committed to changing the world as I had been during my involvement in the antiwar movement. At that time, in 1975, the police in the small town where I lived were trying to acquire machine guns to repress those remnants of the antiwar movement they felt were subversive. The police were becoming like a military unit, which was not right. I became involved in an effort to keep machine guns out of their hands.

I had read the autobiography of Malcolm X while I was on retreat, and I became convinced that the revolution was in prison and that I had to connect with prisoners.

I was first exposed to the Black Panthers at a soul food feast in Toledo, Ohio. I was fourteen. After Martin Luther King was assassinated, the Panthers had advocated picking up the gun. The idea of self-determination for African-Americans was in the air. I saw a poster of Huey P. Newton seated on an African straw chair, his feet firm on a zebra skin, the butt of a rifle planted on his right side, a Zulu spear in his left hand. I was smitten. Terrified, I suppose, but also thinking that maybe I had been born to the wrong race. Embarrassingly the utter stereotype, I was the original wannabe and perhaps the palest black revolutionary that ever lived. And the goofiest.

When I was a young father in the early 80s, the Panthers ran a free food program in Oakland to feed children and old folks. I'd bring them wild mushrooms and go to supermarkets where fruits and vegetables that were a little old or cheese that just needed a little mold cut off were being thrown away. I'd go to the fields outside of town and gather artichokes and onions left behind after harvest. When you've been hungry, you become an expert in gleaning and gathering.

At the same time I began writing to prisoners who claimed they were members of the Black Liberation Army. I helped a couple of them once they were released find comrades on the outside. The BLA was a more militant splinter from the Panthers. The Panthers were founded with Malcolm's assassination, and the BLA carried the disillusionment with nonviolence to the next step: we believed in revolution not only in America but internationally. Ché Guevara was our patron saint. My friends in the BLA were also confused men, very *macho*, as we say in Spanish, who believed in violence as the way to solve things. They were also self-destructive.

My relationship with these men was altogether strange and strained by the mad idealism of a young man. Still, they called me "brother" and we had a very dangerous country to overthrow. We worked hard to tolerate one another.

My main contribution to overthrowing America was being a liaison between prisoners in different prisons and smuggling them drugs. I was naïve enough to believe that the money from selling drugs would go to paying lawyers.

I would make balloon lozenges half a thumb thick, put a dozen in my underwear, grab my Bible, and enter the California Men's Colony as a long-haired preacher boy. Who would suspect anything, right? Once I was in, I'd wait while my friend Andre was told he had a visitor.

One afternoon, Tex Watson, of Manson Family fame who had got Jesus behind bars, was praying at the right side of the waiting room. Andre and I veered toward him because the light of his determined sincerity was a great cover but stayed distant enough so I could crack open Corinthians and preach.

With Christian earnestness I passed the balloons under the table for Andre to swallow with coffee. Praise God! Hallelujah! Guard Sanchez didn't notice a thing.

After Andre had his "meal," we hunkered down and talked revolution—specifically, the liberation of Rhodesia from white minority rule. He said the BLA was organizing a small guerilla army to fight in the war of independence there. They had contacted a woman in the Italian Communist party with connections in Africa. We were going to be trained in weapons in southern Italy by the Palestinian Liberation Organization and then go to Rhodesia to fight apartheid.

But I was the only white person among these men, and it was not a good scene at all. Ultimately it came down to five years of watching people whom I considered my friends destroy themselves. One, Charles, finally left prison after eight years. In prison, he was like the Buddha: so calm and smart, so sharp. We'd discuss Malcolm and Mao. I considered him an elder. The week he got out of prison, he began selling drugs and carrying weapons. After four months I lost contact with him. He was driven either to get back in prison as quickly as he could or to get killed. Those were the only choices he knew. He couldn't stand being on the outside.

This being memoir, I write as if it's true, but the truth of the matter is that there is much I don't know. My time with the BLA was more than a little murky. So let me begin again:

In those years I probably wasn't a member of the Black Liberation Army. Or was I? My friends in prison were or were not members of the BLA. We were or weren't going to Italy to train with the PLO at the country estate of a woman in the Italian Communist Party. We were or were not going to Rhodesia to fight apartheid. The fog of untruth was so thick and I was so eager to be accepted. Was I a patsy? Well, I did volunteer, didn't I? Willingly and willfully gullible. I was, after all, a brother, and being called "brother" meant a lot to me then. But really, who were these comrades in prison? Who was Carlos who trained me in weapons on the outside beyond a tender father and a damned good shot?

And who the hell was Michael Ortiz Hill? An aspiring urban guerilla who could scarcely contain his desire to die on behalf of the poor? Or simply a talented drug smuggler?

I'll never know.

At any rate, this mystery within a mystery proffered a great gift. Day after day I lived with the single essential question: In this life am I willing to kill another? By the time I was able to answer "no," the question had lived in my bones for several years and that refusal to kill has framed who I am.

In this life no one will die by my hand. The question of whether or not to pick up the gun made a pacifist of me.

The irony has not escaped me that when I finally made the trip to Mandaza's country, to what by that time had become Zimbabwe, it was not as a warrior after all. I didn't go to fight. I went to learn peace, and it took me twenty years to get there.

"I know why you didn't fight in our War of Independence," says Mandaza.

"Why?"

"Your spirits are peacemakers. They're not warriors. Had you ignored that, they would have arranged your death and I would never have met my *mapatya*."

11

▼▼▼▼▼

BECOMING A POLICEMAN

MANDAZA: I came back down to Harare on holiday. During this time I was living with my uncle, and he introduced me to a friend who was in charge of a certain police station in Harare. That officer wanted to find a qualified school-teacher because he was going to open a police school. I didn't want to be part of the police force because of my politics. I just didn't want this at all, having been in Highfield under police occupation. But my uncle's friend called a secret meeting to make me join the force without me knowing it. The police force was integrated, but whites wouldn't let their children go to school with black children. They wanted me to teach the children of black policemen.

This policeman friend of my uncle asked me to take a letter for him to a recruitment officer in Harare. "Please, my son, can you deliver this letter for me?" I said I would do it, not knowing that I was carrying a letter that had something to do with me. I took it to the recruitment office, and they just looked at me. They didn't want to interview me because they knew I would refuse to join them.

They listened to me, treated me as a friend, and I listened to them, and so forth. They had already sent a letter to the Minister of Education saying they had found a qualified teacher. They had sent letters to my previous schools asking for recommendations—"How is he?"—and so forth. I couldn't warn my schools in time to say bad things about me. My transfer by the Ministry of Education into the police force was granted without my knowing it. I was accepted into the British South African Police, the BSAP. When I looked at this letter from the Ministry of Education, I thought, "My God, what on earth is this now?"

I stopped teaching while they trained me. The training was long and tough. I had to know the law. Everything. When I completed my training, they sent me off to teach. So I found myself teaching in a police uniform. I didn't like it, but what could I do?

Under those conditions I decided to go and visit some of my friends in Highfield who were Nationalists, members of the National Democratic Party, ZAPU, ZANU, and so on. I consulted with them, and they said, "Well, if we are fighting this government, we are lucky because we've got you in the BSAP. You'll learn a lot about how they operate." This is how I started. I was happy to see how the British South African Police Force operated.

At one of the annual meetings of the black officers with the senior white police officer, a white officer showed his true colors. We were to be addressed by our bosses, the whites, about the conditions of service in the British South African Police. One guy, a black man, stood up and requested information about our pension fund. This white boss stood up, angry and bitter, and said, "You blacks don't ask that question. You are not policemen. We are only training you to be our messengers."

In response to such insults we were trained to say, "Yes, suh!" Whether you agreed with him or not, it was always just, "Yes, suh!"

That moment awakened me to the situation we were in. When we were given some forms to complete, I took them home and tore them to pieces. I didn't want any part of it.

But I had been forced to join. A few months later after this incident, another white boss who was younger—I could have called him my brother—came to the school where I was. He wanted to search all of my headmaster's professional books. Just because he was white, he had to look at everything the blacks were doing. But this was not his school at all. He knew nothing about what we were doing there. He acted as if he had the right, as if he were an official from the Ministry of Education. Not just anybody in the British South African Police could inspect my headmaster's books.

I greeted him like a friend when he came into my office, and he just started looking at what we were doing in the classrooms. I showed him everything. Then he said he wanted to see my records.

I said, "What records?"

He didn't know them by name. He said, "You keep some records here. I want to see them!"

I said, "Mr. Heatherly, you cannot do that."

He said, "Why not?"

I said, "You don't have the right to look at these documents here. The only people who have a right to do that are from the Ministry of Education. You can only come to see whether the buildings are in good condition. That is as much as I know about your duty."

He insisted that he was my boss, and he sat on my chair, saying, "I am your boss, and you will do whatever I say."

Then I started talking to him, and I said, "You know, you are my brother, and I welcomed you here. I know you are my boss because of your color, but just because of your color. Yet when it comes to this place, you have gone too far. I am saying that you are no longer my boss in this room."

CHAPTER 11

He became angry, very cross. "I can put you in jail for saying that," he said.

"Putting me in jail doesn't solve the problem. It will even make things worse between you and me."

"Don't talk to me like that, you kaffir."

"That's enough, sir. I'm closing my office. You can go and talk to your senior officer, or you can take me to prison right now. Lead my way. I will go," I said.

He said he was going to report me to his boss. He went to the police administration and stayed there the whole day. The following morning he came back and said, "Augustine, please forgive me." The next morning! "Please forgive me."

I said simply, "Thank you, brother."

So that's one of the incidents in a long life, a long journey through life. I'll never forget that one.

I don't hate the white man, really. I hated the system, that evil system. I prayed in those days that such a system would come to an end peacefully.

When the British South Africa Police sold my services to the schoolchildren, they decided I should teach two classes in the same classroom, one group facing this way, one group facing that way, and I did that for several years and for no extra pay. They called them good services from a poorly educated schoolteacher. I don't really know how good these services were. Yet I enjoyed being with these kids all the time. I wasn't married. I'd even approach their parents and say, "Can I have them in the evening? I'll teach them for free!" Because we were living in a police camp, the children were often at home doing nothing. So I'd ask teach them in the evening from seven o'clock to half past eight.

12

■ ■ ■ ■ ■

BECOMING A NURSE

MICHAEL: I fell in love with my first wife while I was doing political organizing. Marsha was a kind Jewish woman, a political activist, a feminist. I moved off the street to live with her. After I had been with Marsha for three months, my father died, and my daughter, Nicole, was conceived two months after that.

It was terrifying to live in a house again. I don't know how to describe it except that I felt confined and suffocated.

Marsha had a college degree, and she worked as a school-teacher. Financially, it made sense for me to stay at home with Nicole. I became the "mother" in the family. Loving my daughter and being at home with her was an opportunity to recover from my time as a street kid.

I did not go to my father's funeral. One reason was that I couldn't bear the sadness I felt. Another was that I was ashamed to cry in front of my brothers and sisters and my mother. Yet my shame and grief left me hollow inside and unfinished, so I started doing volunteer work with people who were dying. I found that I liked it a lot.

The first part of my training as a *nganga* was on the street. The second part was working with people who were dying—mostly people with cancer, and then, later on, people with AIDS and other diseases. During that period I had assisted with my daughter's birth and was asked to help with a couple of other births as well.

CHAPTER 12

This was an incredibly rich time for me. I felt honored to be a part of these passages: birth and death. It changed me. I decided to train as a registered nurse.

Marsha was and is a good mother, a very good mother. But I was a boy who had been homeless for years, and I was terrified of her. I certainly was not a good husband. I was a good father, but as a husband I had affairs with other women. I made my ex-wife suffer quite a lot, and she ended up leaving me after seven years for someone else, a friend to whom I had introduced her.

After Marsha left, I was devastated. For seven years I had had a home. Though it was strange to live within the four walls of a house, nonetheless, I had a roof over my head and food to eat. I had failed in everything. I really wanted to be a good husband, but I didn't know how. I was not capable.

In the aftermath of my divorce I would have returned to homelessness if it weren't for my daughter. Between loving her and learning to love the ill and the dying, I was able to construct a life.

13

▼▼▼▼▼

I STARTED HAVING
POWERFUL DREAMS

MANDAZA: Let me talk now about becoming a healer. In 1978 or 1979, I started having very powerful dreams. I could not understand them because I had never dreamt like that before. His Excellency, Robert Mugabe, before he was president of this country, would come to me in dreams. He and Joshua Nkomo, who became vice president, would visit. They would say, "We want to show you greater things," and they would take me to Great Zimbabwe, the ruins of the old Shona empire. "You see this place here in the cave. It was used by the fighters hundreds of years ago. Do you see this place here in the cave? It was used by elders who made the decisions. Do you see this place? It was used by our spirit mediums." Mugabe and Nkomo showed me all these holy places. This dream came to me many times.

I used to tell my relatives about these dreams. They could not interpret them. I was left wondering about what they meant.

Later on, at the end of 1979, near Independence, I'd see myself flying like a white eagle, overseeing what was happening. I would be given messages for Mr. Mugabe about how he must look after the older people of this country, the sick, the suffering, if he wants to rule. But I was scared to go and tell Mugabe about them.

Sometimes answers to problems that had been worrying my family about how we should do things for our dead people would come to me in dreams, and I would tell my relatives.

CHAPTER 13

They would say, "Yes, I know that is a problem," but they hadn't known how to go about addressing it until I told them. My relatives began to question where I was getting these dreams from and what was happening to me. I would tell them, "I don't even know."

The dreams even came when I was working with the BSAP. They were vivid dreams telling of the Ministry of Education officials coming to inspect the school and the books, that they wanted more this and this and this, and I'd tell the headmaster about it.

At one point I went to tell my headmaster that he'd better check some important records in the school because an education official was coming to have a look at that particular set. "They are suspecting that you are not using that set correctly." The following morning at eight o'clock a man from the ministry was there. My headmaster said to me, "Young man, I must tell you there are powerful ancestors working on you. You had better find somebody to initiate you."

Aha! He started a war with that comment. I said he must never, ever talk about ancestors working on me. No! No! But he insisted.

"I don't believe in ancestor spirits!" I said. "They don't mean anything to me. I believe in the Creator who created the ancestors. This is my road. I believe in the Creator, the controller of the Universe, not the spirits you are talking about. No."

So he said to me, "Each time you get dreams about me, let me know, because they help me a lot."

I said, "No problem. I'll do it." But I started having dreams that his wife was going out with other men. I didn't tell him that.

I was a Christian, a strong believer in the church, so I wondered why I was getting these dreams. I was feeling miserable in my life then. I didn't know what to do. But then came a time when I wanted to be baptized in a particular church, the Worldwide Church of God. The leader was a Mr. Armstrong of the United States. This man tried baptizing me in the Meikels Hotel swimming pool in Harare, but my spirits resisted. These spirits who brought me dreams wouldn't let him push my head beneath the water. The moment he touched my head, it was difficult. He asked me if I had repented completely, and I told him I had. So he said to me, "Why is it difficult to baptize you?" I said I didn't know. He tried again. It was impossible!

He said, "We'll try it tomorrow."

When I came back to my home on that Saturday morning, he followed me to my place. He said, "Mandaza, it is better you stop from coming to this church, yet for a reason I don't know."

I agreed with him. After this I stopped going to churches.

14

■ ■ ■ ■ ■

THE SWEETEST OF GIFTS

MICHAEL: Following the divorce from Marsha, my daughter, Nicole, and I moved into a little shack. It didn't have any running water; it had no bathroom. It had a light and a tin roof. At first I was getting food out of garbage cans for the two of us as I had done when I was homeless. But eventually I worked my way through nursing school. I got my degree.

I started meditating a lot. In the ashes of the divorce, I realized the only thing to do was to give myself over to learning to love. That's the only thing that matters, the only thing that has meaning in the long run. I practiced the Buddhist meditation of my father, and I eventually learned to find a calm heart to the degree that I was capable then. Life began to make sense. I wrote a poem to the person for whom my wife had left me. "The kiss of betrayal was the sweetest of gifts," I wrote. Had Marsha not left me, I could never have entrusted myself to the spirits like I did.

After I had graduated from nursing school, I got all of my friends and my mother and family together and shaved my head. My mother and my brother Paul and my daughter all cut off a little hair, and then I cut the rest and shaved my head clean. After a night of drunkenness and laughter, the next morning I once again went into the woods, this time for three months of solitude to meditate and pray. I spent the time watching the animals and learning to be silent. I learned what silence was for the first time. I still didn't know how to live in silence, but I could hear silence.

CHAPTER 14

The old grandfather spirit I had met on my first retreat when I was nineteen returned—the one in my body who was so weary. We became acquainted. I realized he was not me but someday in the far future I would ripen into him. This time he wasn't as weary as before, and he taught me many things. I learned that there was a laughter beneath the bottom of despair. During my twenties and thirties, I spent a total of about two years alone in the forest. Every time I returned there, my friendship with "the old man" deepened.

When I came out of the woods, I got my first job as a nurse. I didn't want to get a job; I wanted to stay in the woods forever. I worked at the bedside of an old woman with multiple sclerosis. Mildred had a hole in her neck so she could breathe with the help of a machine, and she had been in bed for thirty years. She couldn't talk, but I learned to read her lips. We became good friends.

I worked from eleven o'clock at night until seven thirty in the morning. Usually when I came to work, I'd say hello to her and talk a little bit. Then I'd kiss her and put her to sleep. For six and a half years I was able to meditate and pray all night long. That was a gift of God, a great gift. In this life I don't think I'll ever have enough time to meditate like that again.

The first few months of meditating at her bedside stripped away a Catholic hallucination I had been carrying. Looking at her in the dead of night, sound asleep with the nonstop sound of the ventilator filling the room, I imagined I was watching the anguish of the Crucifixion. Beyond that, I thought that it was mine to identify with that anguish, to meet it with whatever dark and hidden suffering I had within me, and maybe become a saint in the process. Then one night, expressing a few hardly audible words through her vocal cords as I plugged the hole in her neck with my thumb, Mildred asked me how I was.

"Oh, a little sad I suppose," I said.

"Why?"

"Nothing really. Life just seems sad to me sometimes."

"I rarely feel sad," Mildred replied.

"How is that, Mildred? Some people would feel quite bitter if they were in your position."

"I just don't let things worry me, that's all."

It was true. Seeing Mildred as Christ on Calvary was just the product of a hyperactive imagination of a never-to-be-again Catholic. It was sufficient to be gentle in turning Mildred in her bed and in cleaning her up after she had used her bed-pan, and to tell her how beautiful she was.

15

▼▼▼▼▼

WATER SPIRIT DISEASE

MANDAZA: One day my mother said, "When you come home, could you buy me some *bute*?" I said, "Mother, I don't like *bute* because snuff is associated with ancestors. I'd rather give you the money to buy the *bute* yourself."

My brother who had a job in Harare had all sorts of ancestor spirits working on him. I'd take him to *nganga*s and tell him, "If you want this man to initiate you, I will pay for it. You go in the house, but I will not go in. I'll stay outside, and you can do your own thing. And when they come outside to pour beer for the spirits, I will say, 'Please excuse me.'"

For years I resisted the ancestors, and with resistance to their call I had water spirit illness proper. The first year I had a problem with my knee. I couldn't stand up. I couldn't stretch it. A dislocation, they said, but where? I went to the doctor, and he said, "There is nothing wrong."

I said, "Look, I'm feeling terrible. I can't walk!" X-rays showed nothing. And then my right elbow started hurting too. The headmaster came to me again and said, "Young man, I told you, these are your ancestors. These are your spirits."

I said, "God created two things, life and death. I'm prepared to take either of the two. If this thing is going to kill me, I'll take it that way." I now know that the knee pain was a message that I should submit to my spirits, but my thinking was: "Instead of visiting a *nganga*, I would rather die."

This went on for some time. My headmaster used to send a driver to collect me because I couldn't walk. Then I developed a flu, a strange flu. I went to see my doctor. He gave me the medicines of the hospital. They never worked.

Around this time I saw my face in a dream. I was dressed in a police uniform with *bute* in my hand. Yes! In the dream I said, "Never! Not *bute*! I'll never take that. If this flu is going to block my nose and kill me, that's okay because I'm still prepared to die."

Then one day an old woman from the village—I didn't even know her—came to me and said, "My son, you are suffering from the flu."

I said, "Yes."

"You've got problems with your knee."

I said, "Yes."

"You've got problems with your elbows."

I said, "Yes."

"I want you to take this snuff when you go to bed. Just take a little bit. I'm going."

And that's it. I took that snuff, just a little bit of it, and the flu was gone, immediately. When the spirits wanted some more, I'd take a little bit. That's how I started taking *bute*. That resistance—gone!

But then something new developed. When I was sitting in my office at work from eight o'clock in the morning to about twelve o'clock noon, I started feeling as if I had to go to bed. I would sleep in my chair and start to dream, seeing various shapes and colors which I did not understand. Some of the visions really frightened me. I saw huge wild animals, big birds, and sea monsters all the time. I asked myself, "Is this because I'm now taking *bute*?" There was no answer.

This happened for quite some time, every working day for months. At twelve o'clock I'd lock up myself in the office so no visitors could come in and interfere with what was happening to me. People would come and knock at the door and think no one was there.

Then one of my staff members, a female teacher at my school, came to me and said, "Headmaster, I have something to talk to you about."

I said, "No, I am not. I'm not sick."

She said, "You have a terrible heartbeat."

That was true. It was so.

She said she wanted to take me to a medium spirit. I resisted for three weeks, but things were getting worse for me. I definitely thought I was going to lose my job this time because I was always sleeping at work.

So we went to this woman who was a spirit medium. When she saw me, she laughed. She laughed and laughed and laughed. I was going to be cross with her. I wanted to get up and walk out of her place, but I continued sitting and watching her because she was trance possessed.

She said, "You are trying to resist the powers of the Creator."

I said, "Oh, yes."

She said, "Young man, you are playing with fire. You will never win. You had better go do this and that. Follow what the spirits want. You are not going to die just because Augustine says he would rather die. You are going to submit. The spirits are with you. They want to make use of you."

I kept quiet, gave her some money for her services and walked out. I said to my friend, "Is this what you wanted me to hear? I'm not going to return to see her!"

I thought I was going insane. At that time I had gone through all the police ranks from the constable rank on up, through promotions and so forth. But these dreams kept coming. I would spend the whole night seeing people sitting in circles talking to me.

Then I saw some people coming from the water saying I shouldn't worry about these dreams. They said the dreams were coming from them. I didn't know these people at all, though some of them came in the likeness of my relatives. Some were women who looked like my aunts. Others were men who looked like my uncles, but they were very old. All the time they were coming from the water, talking to me.

One member of the BSAP called me over to him one day. I didn't know him. He said, "Brother, can you come closer?"

I approached him and said, "Good morning. How are you?"

"You are taking too long with these spirits," he said. "You are taking too long. This is the only thing I can say to you now. Bye bye."

It's not that I was taking too long to obey the spirits; instead, I wasn't responding at all. In fact, after this I resisted more. And the more I resisted, the further I sank into water spirit illness.

I had a car that I used for driving from home to work every morning. I decided to sell it, for no reason. I wanted to use the buses like any other person. Two weeks later, the car I sold was sold again. So I bought it. I used it for some time, and then I decided I wanted to sell it again. Some of these ancient spirits, the *mhondoro*s, they hate cars.

Finally I began to go down. Each month I was getting two hundred dollars, but it started to disappear bit by bit until finally I had no bank account. I couldn't work well. I'd sleep all the time and have nightmares. So I started visiting *nganga*s. I wanted to see if anyone would initiate me.

16

■ ■ ■ ■ ■

THE PICTURE OF BEAUTY

MICHAEL: Let me say a few words about my second wife, Deena. Deena is the one who's going to be with me until I see her off to the grave. We have a deal between us—she gets to die first. She's twenty years older than me, so chances are that's the way it will go.

When I was still married to my first wife, I had a dream about making love with a woman who was much older than me. I was just twenty-three years old. I told my friend David this dream, and he smiled. "Well, I suppose you will have to do that someday, won't you?" I felt at that point that I was meant to be with a woman who was older.

After I had been meditating for five years at the bedside of my patient Mildred, it was time to bring the part of me that's a monk together with the part of me that loves women. I wanted to see if sexuality and spirituality could be compatible. Deena had written a wonderful article about that very thing called "Revamping the World." She's a feminist writer, a poet, a novelist, a thinker, and a fine healer.

I wrote a twenty-eight-page letter in response to her article. The article itself was only a few pages long. I decided I was going to court her with my intelligence. Of course, she didn't know me at all, but at the end of my letter I wrote, "P.S., I think the two of us should be lovers."

I didn't know that Deena had spent a year and a half of her life being stalked by a man. I did not know the violence she had suffered at the hands of men. A stranger writing her a letter saying maybe she should be his lover was hardly something she was excited about. She says she thought I was probably an axe murderer, at best.

I was patient. I knew we were supposed to be together. A year later we finally met through a mutual friend and got along quite well. We had breakfast together, a little coffee, and I said, "You know, in my deepest heart, I think you and I should be together." That was our first meeting.

She responded, "Well, that seems more possible, now that I've met you, but your letter really frightened me."

In spite of the shaky start, we fell in love. She was writing a novel called *What Dinah Thought,* about Israel, about Jews and Palestinians, and she gave me the manuscript to read before it was published.

I wrote her a two-hundred-page letter in response. Turning over every little sentence she had written, I told her how the words revealed her soul. Of course she fell in love with me. I was relentless.

We've been together for twenty years now. I am now the same age she was when she took this waif for a husband! Aside from being twenty years older than me, she is one-breasted. She lost a breast to cancer. When I first met her, she was frightened that I would not find her beautiful. But in truth, she is the picture of beauty to me. I love her so much. She is such a good teacher and friend.

Nicole is also the picture of beauty, also a good teacher and a friend. She is now older than I was when she was born. Incomprehensible! And she is such an adult—tough-minded, soft-hearted, and gorgeous.

I was a child when she was born, a rather frightened child, to be honest. Layer by layer, answering what her soul seemed to call for, I learned to be a father—a man and an adult. This is her gift, that someone such as I would become a man.

Nicole's passion and vocation are acting and directing. Sometimes I laugh with her, tell her that she couldn't have avoided it. When she was born, I was such a wreck of a human being, I decided to read books on acting so I could puzzle out the role of being a reasonably good father.

A few weeks before I first traveled to Zimbabwe to be initiated, Nicole and I went to Santa Cruz Island off the coast of Santa Barbara, California. It was time for her to leave home for college, so both of us were at crossroads in our lives. Of course I wanted to extend a father's blessings to her, but I also felt compelled to confess my concerns that I might have wounded her when she was a little girl, growing up as she did with a father who was thrown here and there by his spirits.

Our first night on the island, she read to me what she had written that day in her diary. I remember the words exactly: "My dad seems to think he was a bad father. All I can think to say to him is, 'Here I am.'"

She is such a teacher and a friend. Sometimes when I'm taken by narrowness or hardness of heart, Nicole quietly reminds me of the values I raised her by, and I remember to keep faith with them.

17

▼▼▼▼▼

THE COMING
OF THE SPIRITS

MANDAZA: I visited so many *nganga*s, so many in Harare, around Harare, each one claiming that he was going to be able to initiate me. They all failed, and I was paying them money. My spirits smelled arrogance and they just wouldn't respond. That was how my money started disappearing, and I was left with nothing, absolutely nothing.

In 1985, I met a young man named Smart who came from Gokwe. He was an Apostolic Church member, a prophet. He saw my problems in his visions, and his spirits said to tell me I shouldn't go to any of these *nganga*s. I asked why, and he said, "Now I don't see anyone who can help you. You are not ready. But the time will come, and you will see someone who will help you." I could not understand this.

One day I went to a *nganga* in Harare. He's a famous *nganga* for seeing people's problems. He said, "I see very ancient spirits on you. I'm just going to try to help you. I'll keep calling on your spirits to help me."

I stayed with that man for two years. He tried his best. Smart came again when I was at this man's house. And he said, "Augustine, have you forgotten what I told you? How long have you been here?"

I said, "Two years."

Smart told this *nganga*, "If you help this man successfully, I will give you everything I have. I say this because I know you cannot do anything for him."

Three days after Smart spoke to this healer, I had a dream. A voice said, "All these *nganga*s you have been with have no power to initiate you. That is why they fail. You see this old man in front of you?" I looked. There was an old man with a bald head. He was speaking the Ndebele language. Then the voice said, "He is the one who can initiate you." That dream was the turning point in my life.

Monday morning I went to work, and a phone call came from police headquarters to say I was to transfer immediately to Matabeleland. Matabeleland is where the Ndebele live. And look at me now. I'm still here.

Three months later this old man came to my office in Bulawayo. He was just sitting outside on a bench. He approached me very nicely and said, "How are you?" We talked a lot— "Where did you come from?"—that sort of thing. Then he said, "You know, young man, you are not well."

I said, "What do you mean?"

He explained. "You have been having very powerful dreams, dreams that you do not understand. You have been to so many *nganga*s. Am I wrong?"

I said, "Oh, no. You are right." I never asked where he lived. I never asked his name. I had been to so many *nganga*s who were claiming they could initiate me. I thought he was one of them.

For two months I never heard from him. I had failed to be initiated in Harare. I didn't want to start failing in Matabeleland too! I'd done what I could, and I decided not to worry myself. I'd just sit and wait.

Then one day a friend of mine said, "Could you accompany me to see my friend?" So we went to this place and who did we find? There was that old man who had talked to me.

I was ready to admit that I was sick, very sick. He started talking to me this time more profoundly, using his spiritual powers. I agreed with him.

The night before the initiation began, I saw in a dream a circle of spirits gathered in an African hut. Half of the circle was a group of old women. On the other side was a group of very old men. Some had long hair, others were bald-headed, long-bearded, and so forth, but all of them were old. I knocked, and they said, "Come in." Next to me was my uncle who had died recently, the one who had been struck by lightning. He said, "Come and sit next to me."

I sat next to him, and he said, "You have come."

I said, "Yes."

And he said, "We are the ones who have been calling you."

I looked at them all. I knew him and his older brother. The rest I didn't know. He said, "We are the ones who have been calling you. We are the ones who are still calling you."

When I looked at them all, I fell down and started weeping. I wept for a long time, and when I woke up the following morning, I was in tears.

I went back to the old man and told him this dream. He started initiating me.

There is a difference between how the Shona are initiated and how the Ndebele people are initiated. The Shona like it to be done with the bringing of beer, playing the thumb piano—called the *mbira*—drum beating, and so forth. With the Ndebele people, it's a more vigorous initiation. One dances until one is very tired, exhausted. One has to do physical exercise in preparation for the coming of the spirits.

The reason the Ndebele want everyone to dance is because they are warriors. Take my little boy Moses—here in Ndebele we will take him out into the bush to dance and exercise to be prepared for whatever might come in the form of war. The Shona were not like that. That's why we were attacked by the Ndebele. We were not physically strong.

You find among the Ndebele some people who have no dancing spirits. My wife, Simakuhle, though she is Ndebele, has dancing spirits and also spirits that don't like dancing at all. The Ndebele man who initiated me saw right away that my spirits didn't want to dance.

One thing I noticed about this type of initiation where one is to be vigorous in dancing and so forth is that it is very difficult for the people with water spirits, like me. They cannot be initiated that way at all. The way I learned to deal with people with water spirits is different. They are to be initiated quietly, peacefully. If these people are initiated this way, their spirits will come. They sit in this room quietly, meditating, smoking, or eating herbs, and quietly go into the water to pray. Water spirits are spirits of peace, so I initiate those people in a peaceful way.

The old man initiated me for two years. I was told in a dream that he had finished his work with me.

"Young man," he said, "you are going to be a great healer. You are going to serve a lot of people. But don't be afraid. Your spirits are with you."

These were the last words he said to me.

When I reflect on that dream about being initiated by an Ndebele, it is clear that peacemaking spirits brought it to me. They wanted peace between the Shona and the Ndebele, a Shona man to be initiated by an Ndebele man.

He also had a dream that after he initiated me, he was to be initiated by me as well—by a Shona man. And when I did that, his spirits came through for the first time in him. So this was the bridge between the Shona and the Ndebele.

When my ancestors were still living, they didn't like violence. They wanted peace. I was told by my own elders that they would accommodate any people and care for them. When they saw war between blacks, they would say, "What is this now? We used to live peaceably with our neighbors." Maybe the ancestors saw why there is conflict between the Shona and the Ndebele people, what caused it in the first place. This is maybe why they suggested I should be initiated by an Ndebele.

I was going to be transferred back to Harare, but the people in this community went to pray to the mountains and said, "Why do you want this man to return to Mashonaland?" They prayed hard.

Instead of my being sent back to Harare, my spirits said, "No more." I'm staying in Matabeleland and not because I want to but because my spirits say so. This is a sign of reconciliation because the two sides have seen the cause of the conflicts. Now we have planted the heart that can expand in all directions without divisions.

The Ndebele people, the Zulu people, the Bushmen, the Tswana of Botswana—these are my immediate relatives now. I love them, and they love me. Their spirits love me, and I also love their spirits. All these people and their spirits are saying, "Here is your home." This is Zimbabwe. Zimbabwe shouldn't have any divisions at all. What for?

I experience peacemaking through my work. I do not say, "I can make peace"; it is the spirits that make peace. With the spirits, there are no divisions.

There are spirits that work through people to divide one tribe from another. There are spirits who work through people to unite us all. It depends on what spirits you are listening to. The spirits I am listening to are the peacemakers.

The warrior spirits are there to protect the peace-loving people from the bad spirits, the *ngozi*, that influence people to fight and destroy others. The *ngozi* spirits, for example, can destroy a whole family, just for the love of doing it.

The warrior spirits that are upon me fight evil spirits to protect the community. So many peace-loving people are in this country. They are the ones who can be protected by the warrior spirits. The warrior spirits I have myself. If you attack them, they retaliate. If you don't attack, then there is peace.

When I was initiated by the Ndebele-speaking man, my spirits came to him in his dreams saying, "We are the spirits that are on Mandaza." They told him before I was sent down to Matabeleland. The Shona and Ndebele spirits had had their own conference. When I arrived, the spirits had already made their resolutions and were ready waiting for my initiation.

The same thing with Michael—he had a dream several years back about meeting me in Africa. That is how the *mapatya* thing started. The spirits are hungry for reconciliation between their children.

My initiation by this Ndebele man, this so-called enemy, was a blessing in disguise. I was being taken to my true home in Bulawayo among the Ndebele people. The first few years that I was a *nganga*, I continued to be in the police force and continued to teach. I was placed under difficult conditions. We had white police commanders who were so harsh to the black policemen. This pained me a lot. I was always praying that all people in Rhodesia would someday unite and be one people. When my dream told me that I was to be initiated by an Ndebele man, I thought: how am I going to live in Bulawayo amongst the Ndebele people, given the enmity between the Ndebele and the Shona? It was terrible for me at the time to come down to Bulawayo. How was I going to control the staff at this new school where the majority were Ndebele people? It was difficult for me.

Definitely for sure, when I got here, the staff was divided. The Shona would have their tea in their room, and the Ndebele in their own room. But when I came to the school, I simply listened to their problems. I talked to them in a fatherly way, and, to my surprise, eventually we were all having tea in one staff room. I came to the Ndebele-speaking people with the question of how we should develop the school. That seemed to heal the divisiveness.

When I left that place, there was true unity. I was received with warm hands by the Ndebele people. In some ways, more than anything, my police work with the Ndebele prepared me to be initiated by an Ndebele man.

Soon after initiation, I started dreaming that I was sitting on the edge of a big river looking into the water. After a moment, different types of herbs would come floating on the water in such a way that I could look at them and admire them fully. I would call them in the dream "my flowers." The whole night they would appear like that, different types.

Among my flowers I would see a woman who looked like a fish. The herbs were like hair, long hair. She asked me, "Are these your flowers?" And I said, "Yes." "Go," she told me. "Collect them from the river and bring them to your home."

The first three days I had this dream, I'd say, "What are these flowers here?" because I didn't like to handle flowers at all. The dreams kept coming. I went to a river near where I was living and picked a few, just a few, and took them home.

The mermaid came again in a dream and said, "We are not learning to heal. We were born healers. I want more of those herbs." My own spirits were coming to talk to me after the initiation: "We were created healers. We are great healers. Go and get our herbs. Prepare these herbs this way, this way, this way." So I started doing it.

Then an old man came, but he had wings. He lived in the forest alone. He was busy boiling herbs in clay pots. Some of his herbs were drying on rocks, and others were already powdered. He was pounding some herbs, preparing them. I went to his place accompanied by this mermaid and watched him. He never talked to me. He only talked to the mermaid, and I didn't understand what they talked about.

The old man came to me again in the next dream to show me other herbs, not from the water this time but from mountains and forests. He said, "These are my herbs. I am a great healer."

That mermaid is the one I call Ambuya Grandmother Chop-chop because she is fast, efficient, that one. She owns the herbs in the water and along rivers and lakes. The old man is an earth spirit. His are the herbs of the forest and the mountains. The two of them taught me how to mix the herbs so that my medicine has the power of water and earth. They came to show me that I was to be a *nganga* who uses herbs. I was surprised by this.

This is how I started collecting herbs. The spirits showed me how to use them, when to use them, how to prepare them. My spirits are doing it the way they like. This is how I became a healer. It was not through training by anybody. I became a healer after initiation the way the spirits wanted.

18

■ ■ ■ ■ ■

WHILE THE CITY BURNED

MICHAEL: I flew into Los Angeles to be with my wife and a friend who was dying of liver cancer at the time when Los Angeles burned in 1992. A fellow named Rodney King, a black man, was pulled over in his car by four white policemen and beaten to a bloody pulp. This is not unheard of in this country. However, this time there was somebody across the street with a video camera, and it was caught on film. The policemen were brought to trial, yet the white jury, in spite of the video evidence of clear police brutality, voted the police innocent.

Folks call it an uprising or a riot. For me, it was heartbreak. Some people in the black community rioted and started lighting the city on fire. But it wasn't only black people; Mexicans and white people also rioted. People were outraged. I was flying into Los Angeles when it was burning, and we couldn't get into the city. The skies were so filled with smoke, the planes couldn't land. What was supposed to be a one-hour flight took six hours. When I finally arrived, Deena drove me directly to the house of our friend Hella, who was on the edge of death.

In the middle of the fire, in the middle of the riot, this woman had one of the most beautiful and peaceful deaths I have ever seen. Hella died tenderly in her son's arms at two in the morning.

The next morning I walked through the streets of the city. Shattered glass was all over the place. I passed a black woman on the street. I could feel the distance between us. She had ash on her body and was disheveled. She could not look me in the eye, and I could not look her in the eye. A gulf was between us, and there seemed to be no conceivable way to reach across it.

I returned to Hella's house. They had taken her body away. Our friends had poured good wine to drink to celebrate the life of this woman who had died so well. When one of the police helicopters flew overhead, I started weeping about the world that my daughter was growing into. I wanted more than anything to know what I could do to heal this world—to lay hands upon it, to allow it to break my heart, to let Spirit break in, to yield to Spirit, and to find the courage to act.

19

▼▼▼▼▼

INDEPENDENCE

MANDAZA: The ancestors were involved in the winning of our freedom. Without them the apartheid would be with us to this day.

During the second Chimurenga War, my brother actually wanted to go and join the freedom fighters. He traveled from Harare to Mt. Darwin, far east near the Mozambican border where my mother's relatives live. When he got there, my uncle took him to see the guerillas.

In order for a young cadre to join the liberation struggle, he had to visit a spirit medium. The guerillas took my brother to the medium, and she said he must not fight because he had a spirit that had fought the whites in the last century. He was to operate spiritually, so the spirit in him could guide fighters out in the bush. He asked what would happen if he joined the guerillas, and the medium said, "You and these men will be shot." So they sent him back to Harare.

While my brother was off in the bush with the liberation forces, I didn't know where he was. I went to his wife, and she didn't know either. This touched my heart a lot. I prayed hard all week.

During that week my father came to me in a dream. He was sitting on a big rock, smiling at me. "Where is your brother?" he said. "If you had come together, I would tell you many things. Go and find him!" Then he disappeared.

My brother came back, of course, but that was the first and only time I ever saw my father in a dream.

The coming of independence in 1980 was the birth of new life in this part of the world. We wondered: Are we really going to experience true political independence? The whites had reigned for a hundred years. Was it possible that an African could take over and bring us true peace? At first I thought the whites were trapping the blacks. I thought that when the Freedom Fighters came out of the bush, the whites would get hold of them under the pretext that there was to be independence and majority rule. I watched this situation carefully, but it came, independence came! The liberation was real. Freedom was there. We were allowed to go into white-owned shops now. We were allowed to move around freely on the streets where there were white families. But I had lived under colonialism since my birth, so still I thought: "This can't last. This is going to change someday. Look at how uncomfortable the whites are when they ride a bus with blacks on it."

We saw some real changes in the police force. You would see white police officers talking to blacks for the first time as if they were their friends, but we tried to resist their wanting to come and associate with us. I could even take snuff at work, which was a thing never heard of under colonial rule. Before, under apartheid, it was considered evil to do the healing spiritually, following the ancestors. Since people used the *mbira* to call on the spirits, it was considered evil, and we could play it only in our own homes. You had to do it privately. If you were detected, that was the end of your career. You could not remain a member of the police force. The one thing that was considered holy was going to church, because the whites knew that listening to the ancestors spelled the end to apartheid. Independence brought the freedom for me to maneuver and do my work with the spirits. After independence I could operate from the police camp as a *nganga*. I had free rein, very free rein. People would come to me, and I would help them. Being a healer, being a *nganga*, working under this new government was entirely different.

At first I didn't want to show people that I was a healer, but people just sensed it. I started seeing things in people's faces. I started seeing their problems and the causes just by looking at them. This went on for a long time. When I told them their problems, they agreed with me one hundred percent. "That is very correct," they would say. They were surprised at how I could see their problems in their faces like that. I was even surprised myself, because I didn't know what was happening in my life. That is how I started healing people with the water spirits. The spirits themselves would say to me in my dreams, "We know how to deal with these people."

The first woman I actually helped was a woman who used to live here in Bulawayo. She had had a dream fifteen years ago about me. After my initiation we finally met. She came to my home, and she talked about her long-ago dream and her sickness. I was listening attentively. Then I started doing what my spirits were telling me to do immediately. I was afraid because I'd never done it before. I closed the door because I didn't want others to see what I was doing.

After I initiated her three times, she became trance possessed, very powerfully, by seven spirits. They came one by one, relating how the young woman had suffered and how they had been waiting for me and how they knew about the powers of my spirits. They told me things I'd never heard of.

So that was my first patient, that woman with seven spirits. It was surprising because I'd never even seen it. I didn't even know how many spirits I had myself. Right up to now, I don't know how many I have.

When I was through with healing this woman, she went to tell others who had similar problems, and people started to flock to me.

When it came to healing, I was surprised because my spirits told me never to charge anybody a fee. I received people who could have paid me for my services. I also received poor people with nothing at all but who were very sick. In a dream I was told to heal all of them. The ancestors said, "These are my people. They are suffering."

I do this work wholeheartedly and with excitement. I remember one time when a blind man was brought to my place. He had one leg amputated, and the disease was affecting his other leg. I worked on this man for two weeks. He got back his eyesight at this place here. Soon he could see everything. Soon he was even able to drive his car on his own. His leg healed up, and he was able to use it. I did the work for nothing.

In the police force, I was doing tremendous healing work that the police recognized entirely. Most of the policemen would come to me for help if they were being tormented by *ngozi* or worried by their ancestors. During that time it was unusual for a *nganga* to operate from the police camp, but with me it was smooth sailing at first.

Trouble started when people who were not members of the police force wanted my assistance. They were coming from the surrounding townships. Hundreds came each day. The main gate was manned by a police official. Not everyone was allowed in the camp, so there was trouble at the main gate.

"Where do you want to go?"

"To Augustine."

The next one: "To Augustine."

The whole day, people were saying, "To Augustine." And through the weekend as well. All of this was written down in a book: your address, where you come from, where you are going, who you want to see.

The whole book was almost full of Augustine, Augustine. Then the senior police official said, "This is a problem now. What are you going to do?"

I said, "I don't know."

He said, "You are a *nganga*?"

I said, "Oh, yes. I am." I was also a chief inspector by then, a high rank in the police force in Zimbabwe.

He said, "Why can't we do it this way? You work with members of the police force only and leave out the rest of the people."

"If this is what you want me to do, you put a signpost at the gate there—you, not me. Tell the public they are not allowed to be healed by Augustine."

They gave orders to the young boy who manned the gate: "Whoever is not a policeman is not allowed in."

There was a big gathering outside of people who had come one by one to see me. They said, "If this is the case, we are going to report this to the *Chronicle*, to the newspaper. Augustine does not belong to the policemen. He is for everybody."

In that group there were Ndebele people, Shona people, and people of other tribes. They all said, "This is what we are going to do. We are going to demonstrate." So they lay face down on the ground.

At first the police said, "For now, let him operate." But soon the senior police official said, "Either you find a house somewhere else or you stop operating as a *nganga*."

I said, "It is impossible for me to stop operating as a *nganga*. I did not apply to be a *nganga* at all." He laughed because he knew what I meant.

I got a house in one of the townships with a small room, but it wouldn't do. Then I came to this place at 33 Investon Road. The woman who owned the house was also one of my patients. She said, "I think I've got better premises for you to operate from." I worked from that house for quite some time.

While all this was going on, I was told I was to be transferred from Bulawayo back to Harare. It was quite a promotion. I was to have more salary and more allowances because I would be traveling from province to province. I was to be in charge of all the police schools in the country.

A man came from Harare to take over my job. He came to look at the new stations. I showed him everything for a week. He was to begin the takeover the following Monday, but on Sunday I had a dream. My spirits came and said, "Tomorrow, Monday morning at eight o'clock, you go and complete the resignation forms. You are no longer going to be a policeman. We want you to do our work only. Go and do that Monday morning." The dream came three times. And in that dream I saw myself going to the first office with my resignation forms and saying, "Please sign here. I am leaving."

I did exactly this. Two days later they called me and said, "How on earth are you going to tell us that you are resigning!"

I said, "That's final, sir. Please put your signature here."

They phoned Harare, they phoned here and there. I said, "Please, I want your signature. I'm leaving."

They did it. So I left the police force. I should be in Harare right now. Right now! But the spirits wanted me among the Ndebele people. This is my work. This is my home.

20

■ ■ ■ ■ ■

RECEIVE THE DEAD MEAT
FROM MY HEART

MICHAEL: Is it possible to speak a little of those four fierce and ecstatic years leading up to initiation? We'll see.

The process began in earnest one day three months after the Rodney King verdict. My heart was still shaken by those days when the city had burned. I'd begun gathering racial dreams from blacks and whites, trying hard to truly imagine black culture, even trying to understand the African world that had given birth to African America. My book on apocalyptic dreams had just been published, looking at the patterns among dreamers that revealed a "geography of apocalypse." What might racial dreams say about the "geography of race" in America?

I was having coffee at a burger joint in West L.A. At the table next to me a young white man, maybe twenty-eight, cold and faceless, was doing a legal deposition of a middle-aged black fellow, something about a sleazy deal recruiting inner-city athletes for college teams.

The black man suddenly asked candidly for the younger man's assessment. "What do you make of all this?" His voice conveyed some weary desire to be seen and, I thought, for black reality to be recognized.

The white man spoke with no discernable emotion. "This is a legal procedure. What I make of it is not relevant."

"But you have no feelings?"

"Not relevant."

How many more days, even decades, of fire and rage were being seeded by this utterly predictable interaction, just one of many happening across the city that day alone?

I went home crazed and suddenly famished, grabbed stewed chicken cold in my hands. Drank, God knows, maybe half a liter of rum and soon found myself in a flux between gushes of tears and raucous laughter. Tears from the endless violence of white supremacy and the endless violence it gives birth to and the utter impossibility of what I thought I had been called to do—make a bridge across a chasm of history and violation, to find the way of peacemaking in such a world.

Gushing. Pouring it all out. I heard a voice almost audibly, taunting, "Whassup with the blues song, white boy?" The voice was precise, cutting to the quick my efforts at mining self-pity and that kind of melodrama that requires no audience.

The flash of it, direct, sardonic, piercing. And once I took it in, the tears shifted and I began pouring out laughter, knees-weak, gasping, painful laughter.

The voice spoke again. "Whatcha laughing at, white boy?" The laughter turned and became another wailing storm of tears. The voice intervened once more: "Whassup with the blues song, white boy?" and I switched again. And so it went back and forth the whole night.

This spirit that so enjoyed poking fun at my antics I knew even then to be Eshu Elegba, that aspect of God the Yoruba say is the one that tends the crossroad, messenger between the Divine and human, opener of the way of the mysteries.

This event came near the end of my psychoanalysis—months that were marked as a borderland between the psychoanalytic and the African way of knowledge. To make such an epistemic transition *requires* breakdown after breakdown, just as psychoanalysis does when the patient begins glimpsing the vastness of what has been unconscious. Indeed, entering into the African mysteries required a breakdown of the psychoanalytic frame, replacing psychic interiority with a radical and primordial sense of community. But beyond a breakdown of cultural assumptions, this transformation called for a reweaving of myself into a tribal relationship with the natural world, a recognition that nature was fundamental to the community into which I was born.

It was two encounters with lightning that invited me into this mindset.

One day during the last few months of my psychoanalysis, I found myself again in the wild borderlands between two ways of seeing. I paced a wide circle around our rural house, leaving offerings to the four directions. To the west I laid out beef heart and red wine for Shango, the Yoruba spirit of fire and lightning. As I poured the wine, lightning flashed perhaps a half a mile away across the mountains.

That moment was pivotal and remains so. It was nothing so silly and egotistic as, "I caused that." Rather, a door opened to a new understanding: that the soul is implicitly in dialogue with the elements and that ritual can open an exchange. As Deena would say, "What is the nature of the universe that such a thing could happen?"

What indeed?

Shango is a spirit of tempering fire. He was once a Yoruba king who was taken by the power of lightning medicine. Such was his unconscious bedazzlement that he drew down the lightning, and it burned down the palace with his wives and children. Mad with grief, Shango ran into the forest and killed himself.

It was a few months later when Deena and I were to visit Manuela, a Navajo herbalist in the far north of the reservation.

I had a new friend, a prominent Jungian analyst whom I was courting with my somewhat exaggerated connections to Native America. Since Manuela lived in a part of the rez where the peyote church was active, perhaps a visit to her would lead to a way for my friend to be invited to partake of the hallucinogen in one of their all-night ceremonials.

On the way to Manuela's, Deena and I stopped to stretch in the Arizona mountains. I had read that the Navajo used the bark of a lightning-struck tree for medicine.

Medicine for what?

I didn't know.

When we saw the long wound in a Douglas fir, stripped and bleeding thick amber, I gathered the bark and sang to Shango. I knew I had a special gift for Manuela. She would know its use.

Also, and far, far darker, I imagined my gift as a bribe of sorts for connections to the Native American Church and peyote.

There are reasons why in Navajo thinking the *biligaana* (whites) are considered a variety of *ana'i* (enemy) one must be wary of.

As we approached Manuela's round mud house, lightning was striking in three directions. And close by, too.

Manuela greeted us with her usual warm reserve, but conversation was difficult amid the endless waves of thunder. When I pulled out my "gift," Manuela blanched with fear.

It seems that while I was singing to Shango, Manuela was at the closure of a two-night lightning way ceremonial for a middle-aged man who'd been struck. The culmination of the healing rite is drinking tea from the bark of a lightning-struck tree and vomiting up the lightning spirit.

I then also blanched. I had transgressed against lightning and against the Navajo tribe in one tricky little gesture: gathering a bribe, denying even to myself that I was doing so, calling it a gift. The rage of thunder shattered my self-denial.

"It's okay," said Manuela. "Take this bark outside now and fold it into the earth near a coyote bush and the lightning will go away."

The moment was hard to read. Either she was confident that I wouldn't get struck, or she was indifferent. Or perhaps, if I was to learn to walk in balance after my suspiciously timely "gift," this was the moment to act like a man.

I found a coyote bush perhaps twenty yards from the house, buried the bark, and said only, "I am so sorry." Within a few minutes the lightning departed far out of reach from Manuela's world.

It was scarcely half a year before I would be in Zimbabwe for my first initiation. My dreams were clear, the calling undeniable, but as I continued paring away my resistance I had come upon this simple bone-headed white arrogance. I still carried the mark of an unseen and thus unrepentant white supremacy with the most contemptible twist. There was an implicit aggression. I had so inflated myself with "courage" to go to Africa and be initiated that I'd forgotten I was to be a guest. I felt I had a right to the indigenous world. A right? As if some kind of ownership? A right to Navajo culture and now to African, myself a little whirlwind of manifest destiny?

It was time for me to break down further. Much further. Did I hang myself like Shango? Well, actually, disemboweling seemed to be the way. Becoming food for the wild ones. On a bush altar I offered road kills with the persistent prayer that God "receive the dead meat from my heart." I'd slice the belly of raccoon, squirrel, and rabbit to feed maggot, coyote, and vulture. Deena became concerned that I was extreme, and perhaps I was.

"I come of the *conquistadores* who made hell for the people of this land," I prayed. "And I come from those who held slaves in Virginia and North Carolina. Strip, dear God, the dead meat from my heart. Strip the greed. Prepare me for initiation, as I no longer know how to prepare myself."

By the time I arrived at the doorstep of Mandaza I expected nothing, not even to know whether I'd traveled across the world merely to set feet on African soil.

21

▼▼▼▼▼

AND THEN THE RAIN FELL

MANDAZA: The spirits said in a dream, "So many people are going to initiate you. The Zulu, the Shona, the Ndebele, the Karanga, even white people will initiate you."

One day I was in the Matopos Hills, and I dreamt I was in a cave and I saw a young white boy running in front of me and then disappearing. I said, "Where is my brother? Have you seen my brother? I'm looking for my brother here."

People in the cave said, "He went this way." I looked for this brother, but I couldn't find him. Two or three months later, Michael appeared.

Michael, my twin brother, appeared after I had that dream where I was looking for my young brother in the cave at Matopos. I thought that I was actually going to initiate Michael, which was correct. And I thought it would just end there.

After I had initiated Michael and taken him to secret places where his spirits asked him to go, it was my chance to be initiated by him. I didn't ask Michael to initiate me, but the spirits had a conversation about this one. They talked. The issue was going to be solved by him initiating me in a deep way—on a deep, more advanced basis.

After praying so hard together, we went to Victoria Falls, called by Africans Moziyatunya, "the smoke that thunders." On the way, fortunately, we had a cassette tape Michael had brought from Deena, who was in America. It was powerful for me, because on the cassette she described what was going to happen on our way to Victoria Falls step by step. It was a time of drought, but she said we were going to meet the spirits in the form of rain. And, just as she had said it on the tape, they appeared. We got out of the car and stood under the showers. She said we were going to meet the spirits in the form of wild animals, and they appeared. Elephants crossed the road, and we stopped and went to meet them. In that tape she was describing things as though she was there physically. Before we came to the river, I said to Michael, "I feel like someday I'm going to meet Deena. There is a call."

At the river, he gave offerings to the wild animals and taught me how to do it. He gave some offerings to the spirits of the water. He laid me down, said his prayers, and prepared me to enter the spiritual world. Talking to me gently all the time, he prayed for me and sang for me, and, for the first time in my life outside of my dreams, my spirits came through—I was trance possessed.

They all came through me, one after another. In my trance possession I saw visions. My spirits showed me their village under the river—a big village, green and blue, with ancestors from every race. From this village Spider Woman, Ambuya Bwebwe, came to me for the first time. The black eagle who protects the innocent came, and so did the white eagle, the peacemaker.

These spirits and others took over my body and took Michael in their arms to initiate him. They wanted to show him their power and wisdom because they were happy, because they were now free.

Before the spirits left, they actually asked Michael to go into the water. There Michael was totally taken over by Spider Woman. The powers that were put into his body were tremendous.

When my spirits left me, I wept. I wept bitterly in Michael's arms and for a long time, because I couldn't believe that Michael could have done such work. I couldn't believe that it was he who had done this work at all. It was unbelievable. But—this is what I thought—there is a white man who is my brother and who is liberating my spirits. It was unbelievable. He had done it.

When his spirits left him, he also wept in my arms. In the end we both wept. I was in his arms, he was in my arms, and we wept. Then the rain fell, a downpour. I think it rained all night.

One cannot liberate one's own spirits; somebody must come and liberate your spirits for you. That is why my spirits called my *mapatya* to Africa. My spirits were wounded spirits, and they needed somebody to do an initiation to heal the wound. Otherwise they would remain suffering. All spirits are from one source. They did not care that my *mapatya* was white. They do not look at the color of skin.

So that is my initiation by Michael, in short. It made it possible for me to come into the hands of my spirits directly. This is very interesting because I never thought in the first place that I could be trance possessed. I operated as a *nganga* for many years without being trance possessed. I was just working with people's dreams and with the herbs and nothing else. I never got trance possessed in my lifetime, except in my dreams, until after this initiation. That is how things started to change.

My trance possession at this stage is different, really, from how other people get trance possessed, because my spirits can possess me powerfully, and yet I still know exactly what I'm doing, even though I cannot control myself. I cannot control my speech, I cannot control my movements, but I still know what is taking place. Other people don't remember anything at all when they are trance possessed. You have to tell them over and over again what was said by the spirits which have trance possessed them. But this is not the case with me. No. I know everything.

Mandaza is actually removed from me. I don't see him. It's rather that he is hidden somewhere. Then the spirits come in and take over. Each time the spirits come and trance possess me, I feel that I'm going. I am being overpowered by these spirits. And I can tell that if this kind of a spirit is coming, it wants that and that and that, and I will prepare for its coming. It's difficult to know how I can tell what spirit is coming. It's difficult because, with some spirits, I know by the way my heart beats. This tells me it's a powerful spirit that is going to come. So I ask, "What do I do?"

It says, "Sit still," and it comes. At times I feel the movement of my chin, and I know the type of power that is going to come. You know, I really cannot describe how it is that they come.

22

■ ■ ■ ■ ■

SO THE SPIRITS
CAN HAVE A HOME

MICHAEL: I was introduced to Mandaza as a *nganga* from America, a way I would never have introduced myself.

"Do you read dreams?" Mandaza asked.

"Oh yes. That's mainly what I do. I also read the Tarot cards," I replied.

I showed him my deck, and forthwith we were sitting in his spirit room. Ten cards, a Celtic cross, the obstacle being the knight of wands. I described the knight, his visionary bluster, exuberant and given to hubris. On the card, he's riding his winged horse, Pegasus. He believed himself an undefeatable warrior until a gadfly bit the horse's haunch midair and the warrior was cast to his death.

"I recognize that spirit very well," said Mandaza. "Can you cast it from me? I can cast spirits out of others, but I can't cast them from myself."

As I was to learn, this was Mandaza's first gesture of initiating me. The knight I, too, knew personally all too well; his breakdown had been characteristic of my own in the months before I met Mandaza. What else would resurrect the fallen warrior quite like making a pilgrimage across the world and having the healer ask that I heal him? The dilemma was transparent. My breakdown had either made it possible and right to cast the spirit out, or it would lead to quite the opposite: the knight within me would "reinflate," resulting in a false, disastrous reality.

III

"I'll pray on it and Spirit will tell me if I'm ready," I said. Before I went to sleep I did so and drew the Ace of Cups saying yes, the beginning of a new story in the element of water.

In the morning I got a knife, some oil, and a candle. I had Mandaza lie on his back, and I oiled him up and massaged deep in his solar plexus, singing a Yoruba song to Shango, the spirit of fire and lightning. The knight is most certainly a child of Shango.

With the knife I sang a song to Obatala, the Yoruba peace-maker, "father of the white cloth." I shaved off the oil and basted a candle with it.

"The knight to Shango, and Shango to his father. Burn this candle as you sleep."

That evening the clan gathered for drumming, singing, and a possession ceremony. A young Shona man trembled as he was taken by a *sekiru* (grandfather) spirit who addressed me directly: "That ritual was perfectly done. We have received the offering. The way is open to you. We welcome you."

The Shona man could not have seen the ritual. He had arrived hours after it happened. The grandfather spirit, on the other hand, saw it all and spoke of it with appreciation.

Mandaza translated, and he said, "He is Shona like us. With us he is Ndebele. He almost fought in our War of Independence." I looked at the circle of black faces and saw kin and was received as such. I had been with the *nganga* merely a day.

That night I dreamed I was on unearthly land, beautiful with distinctive red sandstone formations. There were two moons in the sky and I was to go to them, but first I had to "read" a cave painting: an elephant, antelope, people dancing.

When I told Mandaza the dream, he said, "That is Matopos, south of here. A holy land. The moon is the Mambokadzi, the queen, the Mother of the Water Spirits."

"And how can I possibly read the cave painting?"

"When the time comes she will tell you, of that you can be sure. Put away your cards for now. I'll tell you when you can use them again. Meanwhile read this," he said, handing me a ritual stick.

I held the stick with my eyes closed, running my hand along its length. "I see a river under the ocean, but I don't know where it's going," I said.

"This is from the Seychelles Islands. Soon you'll read your ticket to the moons."

Mandaza continued my initiation. Herbs mixed with leopard fat put in a cut in my wrist, sweat baths, prayers. He listened closely to my dreams. "That's a working dream," he'd say, if the dream was offering ritual instruction.

The moon was ripening, and we traveled north to the Zambezi River and Victoria Falls, Moziyatunya. Mandaza had had a dream many years before that he was to go to the Zambezi and be given healing herbs directly by the spirit. He couldn't imagine what this meant but had driven the six hours to the river. He sat waiting a couple of kilometers upstream from the waterfall and soon noticed a water bird bringing herbs in its beak and leaving them on an island. The river was low with drought, so Mandaza was able to wade across and gather the herbs. On the shore he then slept and dreamt how the spirits used those herbs to heal.

Mandaza took me to this place, and it was here that Spirit came through and completed our initiation.

It seemed so simple.

I climbed in the river and sang gratitude. I'd been received with such generosity by African spirituality and as a member of the Shona and Ndebele tribes. I asked only that I serve Mandaza's spirits. There was nothing to ask for myself. Any kind of spiritual greed that would distort had finally been washed away.

When I came out of the river I laid an altar: two halves of a broken stick, crossed, a little elephant dung, and a flower. I poured rum on the altar and sang to the spirit of the cross-roads. Mandaza lay on his back with his eyes closed and I spoke softly, identifying his spirit with the spirit of the river.

I meditated along with Mandaza for a half an hour, and then the spirits came through him, one after another. For hours. I'd seen people trance possessed for an hour, perhaps—but five hours?

A hunchbacked old healer took Mandaza's body. I had to help him walk because he could barely use his legs. He performed rituals on me that I couldn't understand, chanting, weeping.

The black *chapungu* came, the eagle, fiercest of warriors, riding thermals. He gathered herbs with his talons—Mandaza's hand—and crushed them into my chest.

I allowed myself to be ministered to by spirits. I kept vigil. When I was afraid, I'd sing a half-remembered Ndebele song to the Mother.

"Whew!" Mandaza said. "I didn't know my spirits were so powerful." Mandaza said this, not a spirit. Then, he returned to being more spirits, but I knew he would return to being Mandaza.

When he did, I collapsed in his arms and wept. "There is no cure for the arrogance of a young man except time," I said.

"Michael," he said. "You must understand that this was the first time I was ever trance possessed. My wife has fasted and prayed that my spirits would come, and I have gone to many *ngangas*. But my spirits smelled arrogance and so they wouldn't come. You're the first one to approach me without arrogance."

That night we slept in the car, Mandaza in the front seat, I in the back. I dreamt I was before the cave paintings again and this time I could read them clearly; they said, "This one now has two mothers." That night, I was awed to notice one moon high in the sky and the other reflected on the river. Mandaza had been confident that the Mambokadzi—the Mother of the Water Spirits—would tell me when I was ready.

23

▼ ▼ ▼ ▼ ▼

THE WHITE EAGLE

MANDAZA: Michael returned to Zimbabwe a few months later, and again we entered into initiating each other. I had been prepared for this second initiation by a strange dream back when I was still in Harare before I was initiated by the Ndebele man.

In the dream, I was walking past a big dam full of water when I saw a snuff container on the wayside. I said to myself, "I found myself a good snuff container. I'll come back and pick it up when I return from town." A few steps ahead, I saw another snuff container. Good luck! I now had two snuff containers. "I will come and pick them up on my way back." Then I saw a third snuff container. I said, "Ah! Here's another one." While I was saying that, there appeared from this pool of water three men.

The first man said to me, "Do you know the Peacemaker?"

I said, "No. I've only heard about him and read about him."

He said to me, "You are the Peacemaker."

The second man said the same thing, and I also said the same thing: "No, but I've heard about him."

The third man said exactly the same thing, but this time he told me in a more powerful voice, "You are the Peacemaker."

I woke up, and I was very afraid.

My aunt was there. I went to tell her about this dream. She just sighed and said, "Ah! Don't talk about this dream anymore." So I kept quiet.

Several years later, I went to a spirit medium because I wanted someone to initiate me. The first thing the spirit said was, "Young man, you have had a dream about seeing three snuff containers."

I said, "Yes."

He said, "Things that are coming into this world are great. It is not yet time to talk about that dream."

When Michael returned to Zimbabwe, my spirits said, "We are going to tell Michael what to do about this dream. He'll see how to go about it."

We were at these sacred pools about forty kilometers south of Bulawayo when I told Michael the dream. "I don't understand this one," I said.

He was quiet for a long time and then said, "I know what this dream means, but it frightens me." We did some rituals together, and afterward he said that he wanted to get a couple of beers before he tried to talk about the dream. So we drove back to Bulawayo.

On the way he asked me many hard questions. When we were in Bulawayo, we went to a bottle store and then sat in the car on a dark road talking and drinking beer.

He said, "Now I know why your spirits called me to Africa in the first place. I didn't know until now. They are talking to me, but I'm not sure if either of us is ready to call on this Peacemaker spirit. I know we both have to pray, and we have to go to Great Zimbabwe together very soon."

Right before I went to the ruins of Great Zimbabwe with Michael and my wife, Simakuhle, I had another dream. I saw two white eagles coming toward me from the sky. One landed in my left arm; the other one was hovering about me. I was frightened in this dream. Then the eagle left in my hand his feathers, and I was happy to receive those feathers. I was jumping up and down, excited, saying, "This is a precious gift."

When we went to the top of Great Zimbabwe, the white eagles appeared, not in my dreams this time, but in reality. We saw them hovering above the ruins.

At Great Zimbabwe there is an old woman who is possessed by powerful water spirits. She lived under a river for seven years. The woman had a dream about us coming to see her. She told me, first, that my hair had been plaited for the last time and I was to leave it like that and, second, that we must go to a bushman cave in the Matopos Hills for initiation.

As it turned out, this part of Matopos where she directed us I knew quite well. It was a place where my spirits had sent me to honor and make peace with the Ndebele spirits, where I had left an offering of a snuff container on the grave of King Mzilikazi. And so it was that here I was taken over fully and completely by the Peacemaker.

When we went down the hill back toward Bulawayo a few hours later, I was still trance possessed. When we got down to the bottom of the hill, there appeared police officials who wanted to know why we were there. The spirit told them to remove their shoes and to kneel down, and they did. Through me, the spirit told these men to look after this place, that it should be clean at all times—no waste paper, no fires to be lit around it, no one to wash in the river using soap, no cutting down of trees. "Don't disturb the nature around this place." This is what the spirit told these people. It was dark, and for a long time the Peacemaker instructed these policemen by the headlights of their car.

The spirit said, "This is my place, this is my place, this is my place." Three times he told them. Fortunately enough, the big man among this group of police officers was a kraal head. He was inspector of the group here. He said that tomorrow morning he was going to call a meeting with his own people and tell them exactly what the spirit had said through me.

Then the Peacemaker started telling these people one by one what their problems were and how to go about solving them. They all agreed that there were those problems. They even asked for the address where I lived because they wanted to come for help. This is what happened at Matopos.

In the first initiation at Moziyatunya, the spirits just came and trance possessed me, but they never said anything through me. But this time they were able to talk through the Peacemaker. I am so grateful.

24

■ ■ ■ ■ ■

SLOWLY AND WITH GREAT TENDERNESS

MICHAEL: I returned to Africa in the winter of 1997. This initiation and the months that followed made it possible for me completely to embrace the life of a *nganga*.

We made a pilgrimage to Great Zimbabwe, where Mandaza showed me the secret and holy places that had been revealed to him in his dreams.

One such place was the cave where the Shona kings were buried. High up on a hill, it overlooked the maize fields below, the little villages with their round houses and thatched roofs, the surrounding forest. Mandaza was able to see the passageway between the worlds where the king's spirit returned to the realm of the ancestors, and he instructed me in how to sit on the king's throne among the rocks and give over to his death.

Sitting on the king's throne and looking down over the fields and villages, I was soon filled with a radical sense of benevolence and power, solid and assured. Looking through the king's eyes, I knew I lived for the fertility of the land and for the welfare of the people and the animals, and nothing in me was distracted from serving their interests. Up to that moment, I had not known what benevolent male power was. I had never really been aware of its existence, the world being tortured as it is in all the familiar ways by tyrants and charlatans. Male benevolence I knew. But to be fully empowered yet without arrogance and for the welfare of others was another thing altogether. It was sufficient to glimpse it, to know of its possibility.

When I lay down to draw the king's last breath, the ground gave way to a field of white. At first there were presences receiving me, white wings opening up and softening the passage, but then it was simply free fall into endless space. No bottom to touch, just falling, forever.

When I left the cave, I was able to rejoin the human world, I suppose. Indeed, the following two weeks we were involved with the challenges of initiating a small group of healers from Canada. But, in fact, this free fall lasted for months.

For the first three months, after I returned to the United States, it was as if I were back in the bitter days of water spirit illness: those years on the street and as a young man, those years before initiation—the emotional disorientation, the vivid dreams and hallucinations, the exasperated and hopeless recognition of the depth of my own suffering and the suffering of the world.

Oddly, however, the hospital and the work of the healer became my sanctuary. It's easy to become mindlessly involved with one's own pain until you are with people who are facing far worse, and facing it often with far more grace. During those three months, suffering within, suffering without, life was just a gaping wound. The Buddhists say that compassion is born in the charnel ground, the field where hope and fear have been reduced to ash. It was in practicing kindness that I felt sane.

And yet I was stubbornly committed to a mad project. I thought if I dug deep enough into the fact of suffering—mine, my patients', the world's—then somehow it would make sense. I was heroically seeking meaning, any meaning, but was constantly left with Job's lament. Then one afternoon as I was sleeping off my night shift, a spirit came to me in a dream.

He was a raggedy beggar, perhaps a little drunk. He shouted just a few inches from my face: "You have got it all wrong, all wrong. Stop this search for meaning. You will never find it, and, if you do, you will never be able to convince yourself of what you find. When you look at the suffering, just remember you are looking at your face in the mirror. There is no meaning to it at all." Was this ever clear! The hospital was a hall of mirrors, a sacred place for me to meet myself.

That night, I returned to the bedside of a patient, an immensely fat black woman afflicted with a kind of flesh-eating bacteria. No one knew how to stop it, and she had two large, infected wounds, one in her buttocks that I could stick my fist into and another smaller wound in her groin, quite close to her vagina. Of course, keeping feces out of her wounds was not easy. The doctors wanted to cut into her abdomen to make a colostomy. She refused.

Twice a shift I'd inject morphine sulfate into her IV line, and, after it began taking effect, I'd start the elaborate dressing change. The wounds were packed with gauze soaked in salt water, and pulling the gauze out had to be done slowly and with great tenderness. Then I would change gloves to remain sterile and repack the wound with clean gauze.

It was 5:00 A.M., and the television was on above her bed. It seems they were selling some cream that removed scars. "I'll have to get some of that," she said, and we laughed. Then came an evangelist named Creflow Dollar, who assured us that believing in Jesus would solve all financial problems, and we both agreed we should get some of this Jesus fellow also. This woman was a classy lady, and I asked her how it was that she was able to keep her sense of humor intact, given what she was facing.

"Oh, I don't know," she said. "I guess I'm just a silly person."

Ever since the spirit came and told me to drop my heroic effort to make sense out of it all, my work as a healer has opened up and at moments is translucent. The ground that I so yearned for in those months of free fall is so simple. It seems sufficient to "do unto others as you would have them do unto you."

25

▼▼▼▼▼

SIMAKUHLE AND GEORGE

MANDAZA: Simakuhle had some dreams that she was going to be my wife. She was my patient. She wanted some help. I was married then, and one important thing my spirits told me from the beginning was that I should never, ever go about with any other women. But she was given such direct dreams, and when she used to tell them to me with other people sitting around, I wondered where these dreams were leading. They were precisely saying that Simakuhle was not to marry anyone of her tribe. Simakuhle was never to get married to anybody except me. She didn't know my first name. I didn't even know her first name. I had nothing to do with her in relation to love, nothing totally. I was strict with my spirits, very strict. Whatever they say, I accepted that, and they said, "You mustn't go along with any other woman except the wife you are married to."

So, I'd listen to Simakuhle's dreams. I could feel my heart beat. I was scared of these dreams. It was like this for two, three, four, five years. Then she was told that she should prepare some *sadza* (porridge) and feed me. I said, "How can that be done? She's not my wife at all."

Trouble started at that time with my wife. Each time I went to bed, I would be trance possessed while I was asleep. She could not understand it. She thought I was ill. She told the relatives about this issue, her parents, who were still living. And her parents said, "Your husband has ancestral spirits which are working on him."

She didn't like it. She was a Christian. It went on like that. Finally it came out in the open, and she said, "You are very sick."

I said, "Yes, I am a sick man."

She said, "I don't believe these are good spirits on you."

I was silent to that.

She said, "I cannot be with a man with such spirits. I'm going to divorce you."

I said, "Okay." I never argued with her.

So we went to the courts, and the magistrate asked, "Do you have something to say?"

I said, "Yes. I love my wife. It is unfortunate because I am a sick man. She cannot stay with a sick man at all. My illness is about the spirits."

The magistrate said, "We are not giving you a period of separation because I, the magistrate, understand about ancestral spirits. I am giving you an immediate divorce."

She said, "What I want from this man is the house in Harare. It must be mine."

I said, "Okay. What else?"

She said, "I want everything in this house."

I said, "Okay. What else?"

She said, "Our four children. They are all mine."

I said, "Okay. What else?"

She said, "I want you to transport all these things I have here in Bulawayo for me to my house in Harare."

This I did. I approached a moving company, and they moved everything. Everything, including some of my clothes. And when it was done, I said, "Have you taken everything that you want?"

She said, "I want maintenance for these children."

I said, "How much do you want?"

She went to court and said, "I want your pension."

I said, "Fine. Please look after my children. Goodbye."

Simakuhle's dreams became more powerful. They were directed to me, saying, "This woman was not for you at all. Look at her heart. We are giving you a wife. She is a sick woman. She is a poor woman. This is your wife for life." That is how we came to be.

She was sick, Simakuhle. She was going to go to the hospital and have a heart operation, so I took her. We comforted one another. She supports the work that I do very much, and I support her spiritually. That is how I got Simakuhle into my house, and that is how I found myself in Simakuhle's home as well.

The spirits have given me Simakuhle not only as my wife but also as my sister. Instructions about how I should work in this community are given to Simakuhle by my spirits and by her spirits. She has the gift of receiving messages through her dreams so that in the morning she tells me what I should do. Because my spirits talk to me while I'm doing the work, they know I need to sleep at night. They would rather give Simakuhle all the dreams so I can rest.

This unites the two of us. No one can do a perfect job alone. One needs some help from other people. My help comes from Simakuhle. When I'm initiating people, Simakuhle has dreams about the whole group. This is helpful, very helpful indeed. Remember that in the Torah, prophets were sent with messages for people. We must have prophets among us to do this work properly. Dreamers like my wife are priceless.

For example, Simakuhle will say to me, "This morning there is going to come a man with powerful evil spirits, and when you work with him, you must put on a leopard-skin belt and use the buffalo tail to chase that spirit away." She'll even tell me what kind of herbs to use. She will tell me these things first thing in the morning, and twenty minutes later the man will appear. I just follow what was given to her in her dream, and the work is done.

Often I will go to a village to do ritual work, and, when I come back, I will be told by Simakuhle that I must smoke this herb or that herb because I was handling some difficult spirits. And then she tells me to go into the water.

I can be a powerful dreamer myself. I can dream about what is going to happen to the whole world, to the president of such and such a country, or I'll be told the spirits want me to rest because the work I do requires a lot of physical power, a lot of thinking and meditating. Before I got married to Simakuhle, I was a dreamer, but now things are rather changed because there is too much work on me. As I look back on these years of marriage I can see that her ancestors and mine were married before we were even born at all, and they wanted to maintain that link.

My firstborn, George, also stands alongside me. When he looks at me, he can tell when I'm not happy. He sees it deeply. I can see his face shrinking. At times I can see the tears running down his cheeks. He is getting that something is going on inside of me, but I don't want to tell him how much I suffer for the family. I know I would be giving him too much of a burden to carry. He is young, so I don't like to be open with him. But what he senses in me is my love for my children. He sees that. He sees how much I suffer for the family.

26

■ ■ ■ ■ ■

INTO YET ANOTHER HEART

MICHAEL: A week before my fortieth birthday, I went off into the woods to spend four months alone. I had planned this time of solitude for almost twenty years. My daughter was grown and off to college. Through Deena's son, I'd become a grandfather at the ripe old age of thirty-two: my granddaughters Jamie and Sarah were pulling on my soul. It was time for me to pause and digest what my life had been, what these years of initiation had been about, so that I could give myself completely to the next phase. It was time to meditate and come naked before God.

My old friend Jay Salter drove me down the Big Sur coast of California, and, under the cover of night, we unloaded hundreds of pounds of provisions—food, candles, books, writing materials. We shared a bottle of dark beer, and, after a few awkward words, I separated from him and spent most of the night carrying everything to the bottom of a ravine where a small creek runs into the ocean. I love this particular place. It is where I was first restored by what I now understood were the water spirits after I was driven crazy by my years of homelessness. Indeed, I slept in a cave alongside the very pool in which I had done my rituals back then.

The old familiarity of the huge rocks that had kept me company over a half a lifetime earlier were a blunt and constant confrontation with timelessness and time, the unsolvable riddle that it was only yesterday that I had been a teenager among these rocks. It seemed not a thing had changed, and yet nothing was at all the same. It was clear that the remainder of my life, however long or short it would be, would pass in the seeming blink of an eye. There was another kind of timelessness, too, that of living within the larger circle of the natural world where my life and its dreams are quite irrelevant.

For the few days preceding my birthday, I prepared for my death. As a *nganga*, I'd often taken people through the rites of death, a perfect blend of my training in Africa and the years I practiced dying as a Vajrayana Buddhist. However peaceably I'd accommodated myself to it, I was still in free fall since that afternoon at Great Zimbabwe. It was time now to do this rite completely and without reserve so that I could give myself to the strange territory between lives where the ancestors do their work—to die so young, unfinished, rived with regrets, aware of the tenacity with which I had sold myself short and had lied to others and, most intimately, to myself. I had failed at so much, and yet there was a sad and sweet recognition that I had faithfully approached every interaction with the dogged desire to learn what love was. People knew that was true of me, whatever my flaws.

The need to be honest down to the bone, to forgive and be forgiven, persisted through the first two months of my time alone. This was the closure of a life that I had to learn to love before I could pass beyond it. In Latin this is called *amor fati*—to love one's fate. How difficult that is!

Even after one has become a ghost of oneself, memory persists and illusion enters and so does heartbreak. In those weeks after my birthday while I was scouring my past, I remembered a dreadful moment with a mad woman when I was homeless. In the drama-anti-drama of deep solitude, I entered fully into the possibility that I had raped her. Illusion or truth, I confronted what appeared to me then as a fact. It served a purpose. It allowed me to scrutinize my relationship with women. And so I tell it here as it was then, as if it were true, because of where the illusion took me and what it offered at that time.

How could I not have known? I asked myself. As a memory, the incident had fallen under the category of "disgusting things that happened to me when I was on the street." The "to me," of course, is critical, since rape is something that one does to someone else. I also filed the memory under the category of "sex," which was quite different from "making love" in my mind—sex being about the urgency of desire regardless of the partner, making love being about the sweetness of intimacy with one's partner. "Having sex" was always confusing to me for all the usual reasons, but it was quite distinct from "rape." Rape, I believed, was something I could not do. I was, after all, known for my gentleness. And so it seemed that I had raped a woman, without admitting that I had done so until half a lifetime later.

I will not linger with the ugly details. I will only say that I had pumped furiously trying to find pleasure but soon found myself in an empty space where neither of us seemed to exist. At some point, she had called out "Danny"—the name of another homeless longhair—and I stopped. She whimpered, and I opened my eyes to look at her fear and bewilderment. "Dear God, what am I doing?" I thought. I felt nausea and dizziness spinning out of a refusal to continue.

I touched her cheek and withdrew from her body. She was afraid of the dark. The event was complete, whatever it had been, and I walked her back to the halfway house where she lived and returned to my cold sleeping bag on the edge of town, feeling dead inside.

In that moment, I assume, I aggrandized what had happened as rape and then, accordingly, forgot it. What I did was unjustifiable. I manipulated her, for sure. Like so many memories of that time, the recollection was ambiguous. Yet it was not rape. I didn't coerce her; she resisted nothing, nor did she passively succumb out of fear of violence. Nevertheless, my mind defined the incident as rape for its own purposes.

In the woods I was to be alone with my demons in that hell where I believed that forgiveness was not possible. Yet somehow I had to yield to forgiveness. Somehow I had to find the courage to surrender to God.

I knew that forgiveness would be shallow and sentimental if I didn't dig down to the harshest understanding of what I might have done. This was not self-punishing or even self-accusation. I perceived a blindness in myself that could not be illuminated unless I risked seeing myself through the eyes of this woman I had tried to use. I had been sexually violated numerous times as a homeless teenager. I went deep into those memories so I could find the truth inherent in empathy.

During the first half of my hermitage, the woman I came to believe I had raped and those others who had done me violence were my fiercest teachers. With them I tried to cut through worlds of lying and self-delusion. Only now do I see the measure to which I was successful and the measure to which I was not. To the exact degree I refused to forgive those who did me violence I refused to forgive myself, for their faces were really no different from my own.

When my heart finally broke, it collapsed into yet another heart, and then into the continuous music of ocean and stream.

I cried out in the dark woods, wailing without a soul around for miles.

Then came the solace of silence falling like a leaf. I had not known what the heart was until that moment—neither my own nor the heart in which it was enfolded. The need of my own inner work to imagine a victim and enemies had delivered me to the true beginning of a spiritual life.

There is a heart that is not mine, though it lives intimately in me. Yet it could also be said that I live in it or that it lies invisibly among all of us. Outside of this heart I could not find forgiveness. Inside of it, compassion flows. Inside of it I could speak a simple prayer of beginning again.

The starkness of solitude is of a piece with its beauty, and though I speak of wrestling with demons and the hard work of looking myself in the eye, it was actually the absence of drama that carried truth. My days were simple, utterly simple, and there is little that can be said about them. There is no "story" in telling of the rising and setting of the sun, the changing phases of the moon, the intimacy I found with my comrades—the wood rats and the deer mice who would share my evening meals—the passing pleasure of watching the whales swim north from their breeding ground in Mexico.

For several hours a day and into the night, I would sit on my meditation cushion, the breath coming in, the breath going out. At midday I'd pray by the stream and give myself over to the water spirits.

A couple of times a week, I'd gather bags of seaweed and spread it out on the hot stones to dry. After it was dry, I'd go through it carefully, pick out the little sea snails and limpets and return them to the sea. In this way I was able to supplement my evening meal of ramen noodles and canned beans.

There is nothing that equals the beauty of water: the braiding of the stream as it passes between rocks; the wave that swells, crests, curls over, and crashes on the shore. At sunset I'd sit where the creek enters the sea, the tide coming in and pushing against the current of the stream, salt water mixing with sweet water. This constantly shifting boundary where the waters meet seemed to me the essence of holiness, and there was both gratitude and mystery in the knowledge that it might well be years, if ever at all, before I would again see it as I was seeing it then.

A refinement of prayer can happen when one is a hermit, the soul seeking the right words, the true words to address God. In the last few weeks I was alone, it became clear that surrendering myself completely to God and surrendering to the work of healing the world were exactly the same gesture. And so in the afternoon when I would go into the creek, I would surrender to God and to the community of beings that sustains me and that I labor to sustain. "Thank you for having made of this life a gift to the world," I'd pray as I left the water, shivering.

Sometimes I was taken by the humor of the paradox that surrendering all I am without reluctance meant both "Everything" with a capital "E" but also merely this life, puny and forever awkward. Nonetheless, it has its own peculiar beauty. It seemed everything and yet so much of nothing.

There is a forgivable delusion at the beginning of a long period of solitude that one is stepping from the known world of people and community over the edge into a wilderness that is by its nature unknown and unknowable. When I left Jay at the roadside and walked into the night at the beginning of my retreat, I was radiant with this delusion and enlivened by the terror and gravity of the moment of leaving the known world behind. What I didn't understand and could not have anticipated is that returning to the world could be every bit as much a stepping into the unknown, that the world of human beings constitutes an untamed wilderness in its own right. Stepping back over the edge had its own terror and gravity, but this time without the saving fiction that the world could be divided between known and unknowable. Now it was all unknowable, and I was called to improvise the life of a healer within that unknowability.

I recall once asking Mandaza how one tells one's own thoughts from the voices of the ancestors. "Oh, it is very difficult," he responded, "because initiation removes the you that is in you." The "me in me" was quite gone, and I knew it. Sky and stone declared it to me by day, and the cold air and the stars by night. It became clear to me that a self would only be created in dialogue and interaction, nothing less than actually created. It would be only a matter of days until I'd be with my beloved Deena, and the moment I'd open my mouth and enter into the incomprehensible give-and-take of human exchange would be the moment of being born out of the realm of the ancestors.

What a preposterous improvisation of the self—to act as if I had faith when in fact I wasn't at all sure I had the capacity to have a simple conversation with my wife, much less leave the world of the ancestors for the intimacy of marriage. As it turned out, when we embraced and looked in each other's eyes, I cried like a baby and couldn't speak. As we drove north to a rented cabin, I trembled quite a lot. As far as I recall, the only sensible thing I was able to say was that in spite of appearances I was not out of my mind and that she mustn't be afraid. There was a bridge to cross, and I would need her help.

She assured me that I didn't seem insane to her at all. Upon hearing that, I was able to draw the first breath of my new life.

Deena was impeccable—skillful and kind. Between making love and talking, I found that what I was told in the woods is true, that the self is actually born out of the mystery of dialogue and interaction. Mandaza and I know this as twins. Like Mandaza and myself, like Mandaza and Simakuhle, Deena and I are joined at the root. I gave myself a month of re-membering and re-creating a self with Deena before reentering the complexity of practicing as a nurse and *nganga* in the hospital. I had a month of putting a little flesh on my skinny body, long walks in the woods, endless wild and fascinating conversations, lots of wine, feasting on the sacrament of marriage.

It seems that while I was in solitude, Deena had been in her own fierce passage, consciously and generously, hour by hour and day by day, "giving herself away," as she put it, to the community. The parallels between her life in the community and my time alone were far from superficial; both of us had walked the path of surrender. And so she needed me as much as I needed her to help cross the bridge back to intimacy.

27

▼▼▼▼▼

I KNOW IT IN MY BODY

MANDAZA: I came to understand why I couldn't go along with Christianity the way it was being practiced. That element of total surrender wasn't there. People can preach and talk about God or their ancestor spirits in a light way, but when I look at myself and the spirits that control everything about me, the most important thing for me is to surrender totally. I can feel that these spirits are being sent by God and that they want somebody from my family to carry this work. I was chosen to be that person. So I have no option except to surrender my life to this. This is who I am. When I do my work as a *nganga*, I have the confidence that I am doing the work of my spirits, total confidence in them. I also know that I've got guidance from them and support from the most powerful spirit, God. I know it in my body.

In our tradition, trance possession is a revelation of the place where dreams originate. These spirits are the powers that give us dreams. These are the powers who protect us, who can talk to us, who can lead and guide us. They may come through trance possession to talk to the people around you. They have messages for the people around you if you are a healer as I am. Some of the things I may not know, but the spirits know about them. They come and talk to us directly. These are the spirits that tried to come when I resisted. They have the power to trance possess you, to talk to you through your dreams, or even to speak to you when you're sitting like this. Or they may leave you alone. We have to let them come the way they want to come, either secretly or openly through trance possession.

It seems with white people that somewhere along the line trance possession was suppressed by some other power. The whites that grew up after this suppression forgot the way of their ancestors, so the new generation is scared of them when they appear.

This is what I think, but I don't know because I'm not a white person. I can't speak for them. This is only my opinion.

Some African people are afraid of seeing a trance possessed person. I was one of them. The whites tried to destroy the way of the ancestors, our connection to these spirits and to the Word. They tried to destroy the power that supported African people. So it is that some of our people still run away when they see a trance possessed person. And yet it was the tradition long before their fathers or their grandfathers lived. When some Africans see a trance possessed person, they think he's crazy, he's mad. That is why I tried to resist in the beginning. I didn't know.

The second time Auntie Deena came to Zimbabwe with Michael, I saw how much she needed to be connected to her father's spirit and to her ancestors. I understood that one immediately because I spent so many years looking for a *nganga* who would put my own father's spirit in my body. So, just a day after she arrived, I gave her this snuff that the termites make out of wood which breaks down all the obstacles, and she went into the water to surrender to her ancestors.

She didn't get trance possessed, my auntie, but the spirit came. "He had such grief," she said, and she wept. And I wept, too. The violence that the Jews have suffered we Africans also have suffered.

We went to Botswana the next day. Deena's spirits called her to Mandlovu, the elephant. We came to the white bones of an elephant along the road. I saw clearly how her father sat in her now because she left an orange in the bones as an offering and said to the elephant, "They tried to kill my people too. We are peacemakers. We have come to meet you." And the elephants came to meet us that day. That's the way these peacemaking spirits operate—my auntie's father bringing together the elephants and the people.

28

■ ■ ■ ■ ■

NOT DELIBERATELY
EATING SOULS

MICHAEL: Crossing the threshold from the woods back to the hospital was nothing if not dramatic. I was a little frightened, of course, but also bright-eyed and bushy-tailed with the idealism of a healer who was still impossibly young, a nurse who had, with some humor, taken on the role of resident *nganga* at the UCLA Medical Center.

On the neurology floor, I was given five patients, one of whom was a severely mentally retarded man in his late twenties. "Failure to thrive" was the diagnosis, which is to say, he had decided to stop eating. His mother didn't know what to do, so she hospitalized him. We put a nasogastric tube down his nose and into his stomach to pump food into him and strapped his wrists to the bed so he wouldn't pull it out. He had pulled it out already once the first day, and shortly after I arrived, hands or no hands, he managed to do so again. I had to stick another tube in. What else to do? Let him starve?

I do not like sticking things down people's noses—not the suction catheters that draw secretions from people's lungs, not the trumpets we jam in and tape to the patient so the suction catheters don't overtraumatize the cartilage of the nose, and certainly not nasogastric tubes which, when a patient resists, are nearly impossible to advance to the stomach. Needless to say, this fellow resisted with everything he had in him.

For the tube to go into the stomach and not the lungs, the head must be tilted completely forward, chin to chest. I tried to convince this mentally retarded man that the torture I was about to visit upon him was for his own good. I gently and firmly pressed on the back of his head as I pushed the tube in. He responded by arching his neck back while he sputtered and screamed out and spit on me. I asked for assistance from a couple of other nurses, and after advancing the tube for virtually a foot into his body, I was sure that I was successful, that we could continue feeding him.

I was wrong. I placed the end of the tube that was not in his body in a cup of water. Bubbles indicated that it was lodged deep in his lungs. I was afraid that perhaps I had injured him. I'd never seen a catheter extend so far down the bronchial tree. When I withdrew the tube, I was relieved to see that there was no blood at the end of it.

The man looked at me with stark terror, unanswerable and uncomprehending. I placed my hand quietly on his shoulder and sang an African song to the father of light, not knowing for sure whether extending tenderness to someone you have tortured intensifies the torture or softens it. I was grateful to be transferred to another floor before I was obligated to try inserting a nasogastric tube a second time.

I rely on my patients to remind me I am a *nganga* when I am lost in the ordinary violence of the work that I do. Another floor, another world, another little nest of possibilities. My savior that night was an old Jewish man who had just found out that his cancer had spread from lungs to brain. He was what we call a "sun-downer," pleasant and lucid in the day but through the night quite out of his mind.

After midnight I walked into his room, and he was straining against his wrist restraints and crying out. Over and over he said, "It is a terrible thing to die on Yom Kippur." I glanced at his wrist and at the crude tattoo: *kazetzik*, a concentration camp survivor. I remembered the cold afternoon I spent at Auschwitz-Birkenau with Deena, squatting in the mud in the shambles of the old crematorium and planting a few kernels of blue corn. I was surprised that the Polish mud was still thick with splinters of bone almost fifty years later.

"I know where you are," I told him. "It is a dreadful place. I can't make this better than it is, but I can pray with you." I held his hand, and together we chanted the Hebrew Shema, "Here O Israel, the Lord our God is One." In the morning he told me of the terrible dream he had in which we prayed together and then laughed apologetically for wasting my time with such a dream.

I've heard it said that the kindest of the Buddhas live in hell. I know this to be true because I once lived in the hell realms and know the kindness that was extended to me. Suffering calls forth Buddha's mind to meet it: bright, skillful, and generous.

Everything seems to be a matter of crossing thresholds—invisible boundaries that separate worlds—entering the woods or leaving them, the parting of the electric doors of the hospital as I enter in the evening or leave into the cold morning air, crossing an unseen threshold as one approaches a bed of unimaginable suffering or leaves the bedside to the comradery of peers. And of course there is the threshold between Africa and America. I hope to bring a little of the intelligence into which I was initiated back into a world that contradicts it on every level but where I insist that it thrives against whatever odds. Thrives and is honored.

The last time I was in Zimbabwe, the Zimbabwean dollar was worth half of what it had been a few months before. The price of maize went up, and poor people were rioting in the street. As my plane left Johannesburg for the United States, CNN was broadcasting the news of the moment—something to do with the adventures of Bill Clinton's sex life. My heart sank. I was aware of returning to a country that was on the verge of psychosis and terminal narcissism.

My friendship with Mandaza has delivered me to the far edge of the imperial domain that is the West. Economic and cultural imperialism is brutal and predictable in its greed. And part of it is Western medicine, no less an Imperium—no less greedy, no less hungry for territory, no less infatuated with its certainties, no less disdainful of other ways of knowing.

When Mandaza complains of the *nganga*s who think they can heal without listening to their ancestors and then kill so many people with herbs, I think of the recent study identifying prescribed medications as the fourth most common cause of death in American hospitals. These are properly prescribed medications, mind you, given under direct and constant medical supervision. There is no way to estimate the number killed by medications away from institutions, but one could easily guess it to be in the hundreds of thousands every year. In light of this reality, the American debate over doctor-assisted suicide seems quaint: To undergo medical care itself is to take your life into your own hands despite the Hippocratic Oath that doctors have traditionally sworn to: "First, do no harm."

A modern hospital relies so much on the magic of numbers, and by numbers we attempt to heal people: a medical regimen based on statistics and lab values manipulated with drugs and blood products while the person who is the patient is often nearly ignored, a culture of "time management" that has doctors and nurses flitting from patient to patient as if performing purely mechanical tasks along an assembly line. All this is driven by the dollars and cents that the insurance company will pay or refuse to pay for this treatment or that. Numbers, numbers, numbers.

In this flurry of numbers, the West has set itself separate and above the most basic tenets of thousands of years of healing tradition on this planet, which is to say, it has placed itself beyond the reach of the ancestors. We split things down again and again—body split from mind, self from community, community from the natural world, and all of it split from the felt presence of Spirit.

Simakuhle once asked me if there were many witches in America. I said, "No, not really, not people who deliberately go about eating souls, but the country is haunted by evil spirits. The hospital I work in is filled with such spirits because we do violence and pretend it is healing."

For example, there was a young woman with AIDS. She had gotten it from her husband, who had died already, and they had a little girl who was also HIV positive. Tragic as the situation was, this woman had the possibility of a good death if the hospital could refrain from torturing her in her helplessness. She had little pain as long as she wasn't moved. She had an order not to revive her artificially should she die. Her mother was at her bedside. Although everything indicated that she was on the edge of death, the doctor chose to prolong her dying.

One night her "numbers were off," which is to say, she had too much potassium in her blood. The doctor ordered a syrupy medication to bring the lab values into a normal range. Together, we propped her up and pried her mouth open to pour the medicine in. Though she cried out in pain, she was far too lethargic to swallow, and I told the doctor that we were probably pouring the syrup directly into her lungs.

"It is so sad," said the doctor, "but we are doing everything we can for her." As it turned out, this incident was one of the lesser evils visited upon this woman in her final days.

The body is tortured until it has no capacity to resist, and it finally gives up the ghost—maybe. Mandaza says that such a death gives birth to *ngozi*, avenging spirits, and the hospital is filled with them. Mandaza tells me *ngozi* cause nightmares, life-threatening nightmares. For many patients the hospital itself is such a nightmare.

I write these bitter words at the hospital itself, in a cancer ward at 3:00 A.M. I have a brief break as my patients sleep. Already I distrust the bitterness: too simple, too much certainty and thus untrustworthy. Yes, one must rage against the organized lovelessness of any institution, but there are other stories. I confess that part of my commitment to the hospital is that it confounds me, regularly undoes me, shows me the superficiality of my thinking and my loving.

Last week, for example, I came to care for a man the last few days of his life and to care for his family also. He was thirty-seven years old, at the end stage of AIDS with a rare form of cancer that had eaten away much of his face. He frightened people, of course, but for reasons I can't understand. I saw only beauty in him. On my breaks he would sleep, and I'd meditate and pray at his bedside.

Though it was clear he had little time to live, doctor after doctor continued writing orders of aggressive treatment that, I felt, did not honor the moment but seemed to prolong an agonizing death. His whole body was giving out in what we call "multisystems failure." He was confused and had fallen out of bed twice. And so we strapped him in his bed. He screamed, "Untie me, I am not an animal," until we had to sedate him.

I was charting my nurse's notes when a young doctor looked up my patient's lab values on the computer and decided that he needed blood. Numbers! "Why?" I asked. "His kidneys are shutting down. His body is trying to die. What he needs now is to be made comfortable. A little love at his bedside."

She heard me and scratched out the order. "I don't know how you do this work," she said. "I have four patients like him, and I don't know what to do. It is so sad. How do you return to this every night?"

The following night I walked into his room and found him lying in blood pooled around his mouth and eyes, gurgling. I called a nurse's aide to my side, and we elevated him and tried to stop the bleeding from his nose and mouth. We used pressure dressing, ice, and a dab of lidocaine that I hoped would freeze the veins. But we had no luck. We couldn't stop him from bleeding.

I went to the computer and looked up his lab values. As I suspected, the part of his blood that makes it clot was depleted. Suddenly it was me who was arguing for blood. Nobody should die of bleeding from the face. I felt sympathy then for the young doctor who kept faith with numbers, and, although she couldn't bear to look at this man, I knew that she was struggling with the impossible, with how small we all are before the reality of suffering.

29

▼▼▼▼▼

THEY ARE RAINMAKERS

MANDAZA: If you ask me about healing, I have to talk about the water spirits because they are the ones who heal. I do not. I am their servant.

We call on the water spirits because other spirits tell us that these are the most powerful of all the spirits. They say the water spirits communicate directly with God. They are just like his angels. They do not pray to any other spirits in between themselves and God. They have tremendous powers of healing and wisdom direct from the Creator. They are water, they are air, they are clouds, they are rainmakers. This is what I understand about water spirits. These are the spirits that make use of me. It is these spirits themselves who started telling me that they were the healers, and they laid down the steps that I should follow in my healing.

I begin by telling the person, however sick he is, that he should go and talk to his spirits so we can be guided by them. His spirits will talk to him through dreams. My spirits have given me the power to understand the language of dreams, so when people come to me with their dreams, I can tell what their spirits want me to do for them. Then I pray over the water so it has power, and I take the person into the water.

My spirits then say, "You take that herb, that herb, that herb, that herb, which is going to heal that person, who has got, say, skin disease, eye disease, headache, stomach pain, and so forth. Let him go under the water where you have put those herbs."

CHAPTER 29

The person goes into the water. I'm just standing by. He goes under several times, turning over. Then my spirits will tell me, "That's all. That's enough now." And I tell him to come out of the water.

"Let's do some light exercises," I say. Or my spirits will tell me, "Take this patient into the sweat lodge with some smoke and light herbs." When we do that, many evil spirits are chased away.

"Take some herbs to eat with you. If you have any stomach pains, chest pains, what-what, they will disappear with my herbs." Then I give them some more herbs to put in their porridge to work on their blood circulation, respiratory system. For everything they take herbs.

I usually work with a person for three days. After that three days I will tell him, "You go and see your doctor." Then when that person comes back to me, I will want to hear the report from the doctor.

The problem is with people who come from very far. They need accommodations, and our house is so little. And they need food to eat as well. So many of these people who come from far away—some come from Zambia, some come from South Africa, some come from Malawi or Mozambique—they come here saying, "There is nowhere else to go!" So I've got to take care of them. We manage.

The way I operate is: I don't look at one disease in a person. There are multiple diseases in a person, so many of them in one individual person. The disease you may see, which may be detected by the machines, may conceal other diseases that are in the person.

I cure a variety of diseases because I use so many different types of herbs. This water mermaid, Ambuya Chop-chop, shows me flowers, and this Old Man shows me other herbs. I mix them together and feed them to my patients in porridge.

An original treatment, yes. Aha! An original treatment because every story is unique. Then we go into other things. Usually my spirits tell me what else to do, and the person's spirits also will give him dreams on what else to do. So I work with their dreams and my dreams as well. That way the spirits are in agreement.

Sometimes a person comes here who has been having dreams for years. Then all of a sudden the dreams stop coming. I know there is some work to be done there. There is a communication breakdown between him and his spirits. I call upon my spirits to tell me what to do to bring back the dreams, and I give him an herb which is a snuff like *bute*, or I give him just a bit, and the thing that has been blocking him from talking to his spirits will disappear. The next day he will say to me, "I've had now this dream."

The healing that I do comes naturally. You are born with these spirits and then initiated so that they can make use of you. You see all the herbs I have here? Every one of them I saw in my dreams and then went to the bush to gather them.

30

■ ■ ■ ■ ■

CIRCLES WITHIN CIRCLES

MICHAEL: Medicine in the West wasn't always this way. Western humoral medicine, as venerable a tradition as the elemental medicine of China and India, saw that the body is made up of earth, fire, water, and air. At the beginning of the seventeenth century, no doctor would be trusted if he didn't have a grasp of medical astrology. Western medicine had not yet been reduced to technical intervention in a body regarded as a machine. A whole cosmos stood behind and within the act of healing. As in Bantu medicine, the body was viewed as existing within circles of relationship. It has been a great gift that Mandaza has returned me to a medical way of knowing that perceives the circles within circles within circles: self, family, clan, and tribe encircled by the ancestors; the ancestors encircled by the elemental intelligences of earth, fire, water, and air; all of it encircled by the endless presence of God. It seems to me that Bantu medicine is about reconciliation within a field of relationships.

The first time I looked over the edge of the medical Imperium and saw a profound way of medical knowing that was not Western was when Deena and I were taking care of our friend Hella, who was dying of liver cancer. A couple of weeks before Hella died, Deena asked her if there was anything about the cancer that she had never expressed.

"Well," said Hella, "there were the porcupines. When I was a young woman, I was living with my kids in upstate New York, and our cabin was infested with porcupines. I beat one to death with a shovel. We didn't know any better back then. A day hasn't gone by since then that I haven't thought about it. Sometimes the cancer feels like that porcupine poking me with its quills inside my body."

When Hella told Deena this story, I was reading quite a lot about Navajo healing. Among the Navajo such a story would be taken seriously because they view disease as originating when the patterns of beauty, *hozro*, are ruptured in acts such as Hella's. Had Hella been Navajo, she would have gone to a hand trembler or crystal gazer for diagnosis, and she would have been told what singing ceremony might be effective in reweaving her back into the way of beauty, which is to say, back into health.

Shortly after Hella died, Deena and I were in New Mexico, and I had the opportunity to tell her story to a Navajo man. He told me that a rash had broken out all over his arms and shoulders, so he had visited a hand trembler for diagnosis.

Going into a trance, that diagnostician scratched a design in the sand with his shaking hand. Reading it, he said, "You have offended the red ant people." The man confessed that he had poured kerosene on an ant mound near his house and lit it on fire.

Hella's story and the story of this Navajo fellow cast an incident in my own life in a new light. When I was eleven years old and my parents got divorced, I took out my rage on the local insects, especially the ants. I upturned anthills with a shovel or blew them up with firecrackers, and, yes, I enjoyed the image of chaos—dousing a nest with gasoline and lighting it afire.

For three years I had terrible eczema in my inner arms, flaking, bleeding. The Western diagnosis might have been psy-

chosomatic. Some estimate that eighty percent of skin problems have a psychological origin. Had I gone to a homeo-
pathic doctor, she might have celebrated. In homeopathy, skin
problems indicate that a disease has migrated outward from
one's core and is being sloughed off. In homeopathy, it's actually ill-advised to treat such a condition because you risk driving it back in and, in the long run, precipitating a serious
disease. Had I gone to a hand trembler, he likely would have
understood that I'd violated the *wolachi'i dine'e*—the red ant
people—and that I needed a "red ant way" ceremony in order
to make peace with them. Instead, I was taken to a dermatolo-
gist who simply prescribed cortisone cream, which dealt with
the symptoms effectively but had no affect whatsoever on the
disease. Eventually it disappeared on its own, as eczema often
does, as my rage quieted down a bit.

These are three different ways of medicine. Homeopathy
stands at the edge of the Imperium, but Navajo medicine, like
Bantu medicine, is far beyond the edge, as are all the medical
traditions of colonialized people. Native American and African people believe that the natural world is inspirited, and
they know there are consequences to the violence we do to the
natural domain. But such beliefs are at best exoticized or sen-
timentalized, and at worst dismissed as superstitious and back-
ward, by conventional medicine. Rarely are they honored as
real medicine that nevertheless moves on a logic entirely different than the medicine of the Imperium.

Corruption and disintegration occur in Bantu medicine,
too, and it really is no different in its own way from the same
problems in Western medicine. Nonetheless, I have a fond
memory of sitting with Mandaza in Bulawayo when, of all
things, "E.R." came onto the television.

"So that's what you do for a living, is it?" he said.

"Oh, yes," I responded, a little embarrassed at how swept up I was by the melodrama of the program, and more than a little humored at the nostalgia I felt for the hospital as I sat in the house of a shaman.

There is dignity to the work I do, I thought. In spite of everything I will insist that the hospital be a place where I practice the way of the ancestors.

31

▼▼▼▼▼

NOT REALLY AN EVIL SPIRIT

MANDAZA: People come to me to cast out *ngozi*. In English I call *ngozi* "evil spirits," but that's only because there is no word for *ngozi* in your language. They are not evil, but they can be destructive. What they want is justice.

For example, there was a great healer who married away from her village into a new family. She used herbs to heal the people and made a lot of money in her husband's home. In our tradition, when you marry someone who is a healer, you give part of the wages from the healing to her relatives so that the two families remain united and so that the spirit who is upon the healer is at peace. Unfortunately, in this family they didn't do that. They used all of the riches from this spirit and shared nothing with the spirit's living family.

When this woman died, she left behind herds of cattle, goats, money, and other property. Her husband's family didn't want to share any of it. So the dead woman became a *ngozi* in the village and many years later trance possessed one of her own granddaughters, who became sick, mentally disturbed.

This granddaughter came across a man who told her about me, and when she came to me, I saw the problem and talked to her about it. She fully understood. So what I did was to take her to Victoria Falls and perform a powerful ritual. I invited the dead woman to trance possess this young woman because I wanted to talk to the *ngozi* face to face.

The *ngozi* came, and then I said, "Look at this. This woman you are trance possessing and torturing did not commit any offense. She did not do anything at all. What I want is for you to free this woman because I'm going to send her to your village to talk with your people. Then something can be done to make peace."

This *ngozi* wept and said, "You are helping me now." Wept! Then the *ngozi* said, "I will guide this young woman to my people because I can see that her brother is willing to help make peace between these two families. I free her from this moment."

When the spirit left her, I told this young woman what had transpired, and she went to her brother that same day. He was willing to do what the *ngozi* said. He and his mother went to the relatives of the *ngozi*, and they agreed that they should settle this thing out immediately. It was done, and the relatives of the deceased brewed beer to welcome back their spirit. Right up to now, this woman is a free woman. That is how problems with *ngozi* can be settled.

32

■ ■ ■ ■ ■

ALL HIS DISTRESSING
DISGUISES

MICHAEL: Of all the things Mandaza has taught me about healing, what I value most is the way he follows the patients, listens to them, and learns from them—or, in his words, "stands beneath them." I am reminded of what Mother Teresa said: that her work was to serve Christ in all his distressing disguises. I rely on my patients to continue the work of initiation when I'm not in Africa. In their anguish they call forth my spirits, and I am faced with the choice of letting the spirit move or stubbornly refusing to, letting the heart clench.

I had a patient named Jimmy. He was a wino who had nodded out in the middle of the street in a residential district of West Los Angeles. A car ran over him and left him there bleeding. When he was found the next morning, he was taken to the hospital, and a CT scan revealed the intense pressure of blood pushing between his skull and the gray matter of his brain.

A craniotomy was done and the blood siphoned off, but after surgery he caught a staph infection in his surgical wound. It could be that Jimmy was out of his mind before his hospitalization, I don't know. But when I met him, he had been tethered to the bed, hands and feet, for a couple of weeks, urinating on himself and shouting obscenities at anyone who entered the room.

I came into his room sometime after midnight to hang an IV antibiotic, only to find him covered with blood. He had somehow managed to pull out his IV line, and the open vein bled so that he was virtually soaked. I sang a quiet song to myself and sponged him off with as much tenderness as I could muster for a man who was literally spitting at me.

Afterward, I got the doctor to change the antibiotic order to a pill, but of course Jimmy refused the pill. He shouted at me that I was the devil and that he'd be out of his mind to take a pill from my hand.

Who could argue with the accuracy of his logic? For him, hell spread out in the ten directions. To not treat him left him with a raging brain infection. To return him to the street would be dangerous to him and possibly others. In a psychiatric facility he'd be strapped down and drugged around the clock. Such a situation is humbling for someone who takes compassion seriously. Yes, for at least the duration of my shift, I was to be Jimmy's private devil.

When I returned with an IV nurse and a young Vietnamese aide, the sight of us provoked terror such as I have rarely seen. The aide sat on the bed and held down Jimmy's shoulder. I held Jimmy's hand firmly so the IV nurse could insert the needle.

In the face of this kind of horror, it is a learned habit to place hell in parentheses, giving it smaller dimensions, as if such a drama were simply a distasteful task that has to be done during a hard shift. I knew how to do that. I'd done it a million times. This time, however, I chose to keep my heart open in hell.

I closed my eyes and sank into silence, and within that silence I chose to put up no barrier between myself and the raw stuff of Jimmy suffering, to let it wail forth and pass through me and not defend against it. And so it did—a rage and an-

guish in the violence of his cursing that could only be described as the anguish of God. I had never heard such a sound
or, more accurately, had never allowed myself to hear it.

I suppose it's strange to speak of such a man as Christ, but
to me it seems clear—not only the crucified God (myself playing the role of the Roman soldier) but also Christ the healer.
Before my meeting with Jimmy, I confess there was in me a
secret self that was confusing my work as a healer. If I didn't
exactly believe I would save the world, I did think that I would
somehow diminish its suffering by hard work and the extrem-
ity of my goodness. Jimmy healed me of that delusion. He
delivered me to the day-by-day work of serving the sacred in
whatever form it presents itself.

33

▼▼▼▼▼

THE SPIRITS COME IN
SO MANY WAYS

MANDAZA: My spirits seem to like to work with other spirits. That is why I do not know how many spirits are on me. That is why I am trance possessed now by Bushmen spirits, Zulu spirits, and so forth. They gather around me to do the work that needs to be done.

Sometimes the spirits trance possess me; sometimes they come to me in visions when I'm asleep. There are water spirits that come to me in the form of mermaids and then change form. They can even become water animals like dolphins and talk to me like that. Sometimes they come in the form of water birds like ducks and other big birds whose names I do not know.

These animals and birds change into human form and talk to me. And when they leave me in my dream, they change back into water animals and just disappear. Some of them come in the form of wild animals—the elephant, the rhino. When they come to me in those forms, they advance toward me and then change into people.

Some come in the form of sky birds like the white eagle, the black eagle, and the crow which has got black and white feathers. Some of the spirits come to me in the form of clouds. I see a thick black cloud coming down, and what do I see from the clouds? Human beings appear—kings, the queen. They walk toward me, and I talk to them. Then the cloud comes, it picks them up into the air, and they disappear.

CHAPTER 33

Some even come in the form of stars, so bright they come. They approach me from above. They are like little angels. They come close and make a circle, and I sit in the circle. They take human form, and they talk to me.

I see people coming from the water, and they talk to me. The sun sometimes comes to me, but when the sun comes, it's so powerful. The light is so heavy; I almost cannot bear it without being trance possessed. Even when I am awake, they come to me. Some of them come in the form of wind going around me and around me. Then the wind stops, and a person will appear. They will talk to me, and then they go.

34

■ ■ ■ ■ ■

GRANDMOTHER SPIDER

MICHAEL: Mandaza always says that human beings can't heal, that only God and the spirits can heal. "The spirits are God's legs and arms," he says, "and we are also God's legs and arms." Who are the spirits that make use of me in the hospital? How has the hospital become the sacred domain where I serve spirit?

Without Ambuya Bwebwe, "Grandmother Spider," I could never practice as a healer in the hospital. I am utterly reliant on her complexity, her agility, her many minds, and on the subtlety with which she can fold even the most excruciating moments into exquisite beauty.

People who think humans carry the best of nature's intelligence have never watched a spider slide across a web, all eight legs perfect in their coordination and placement. Embodied brilliance at its most graceful, she spins the web of interconnection from her own body and never gets entangled in it. And at the end of a night of hunting, when the web is ragged and torn, she swallows it and recycles it through her gut to spin it out again when night once more falls. For seven years I've looked in every nook and cranny for a living spider to sing to in the hospital but without success. Grandmother Spider is nevertheless present.

My favorite Spider Woman story comes from the Hopi Indians. They say that one winter solstice, it seemed as if the sun had drifted so far out of orbit it might never come back, and all beings would be left behind in the dark and perish. The animals came together in council. Bear roped the sun, but for all his strength couldn't pull it forward a single inch. Wolf tried, but was no more successful than Bear. Finally, Spider Woman with her small voice said, "I can do it." Everyone laughed at the idea of the old woman even trying. But the spider cast a thread through her spinnerets and with hardly any effort at all drew the sun back in.

This story speaks the truth that the delicate gesture of casting out the thread of interconnection succeeds where brute strength and willpower fail. This casting out the thread is largely what I do in the hospital as a healer. As I have moved night after night to different floors in a ten-story hospital, Ambuya Bwebwe has been able to spin a stunning and complex web that has transformed my workplace into a village.

A *nganga* apparently requires a village, or else he is just a cipher among spirits. My cards open doors, and for many I have become the one who reads the oracle, the dream-teller, the one who looks at things from the angle of the mysteries. Sometimes, because I rarely work with the same people two nights in a row, I feel like something of a gypsy. Often I'm embarrassed when someone whose face I scarcely recognize brings up a card reading I had done months or years earlier, vividly remembering it and presuming that I do also. Sometimes it's clear that they had bared their souls to me or that I had shifted their lives in some small way. But when I am the oracle, my words are not my words. The spider knows that beauty is in the making of beauty, in the very act of it, in the care with which she spins the web. So it is with the oracle. It is the act that consumes me and I am not the actor. As I spread the cards, I pray in Shona, making my ignorance an offering.

"*Samatenga tinokumbira!* Speak through me because I know nothing."

As in Mandaza's healing practice, in the hospital the sick and the dying, that community within a community, come and go and call out for kindness. Configurations and reconfigurations are everywhere, always changing. As a *nganga*, I am always entering into them: the presence of this particular patient or family, this specific way of making meaning, this way of healing. It is the spider who comes forth to draw us into relationship to one another, or to draw the *nganga*'s spirit to the bedside. She is poised and alert, this grandmother, always looking for the way of connection, the way of making beauty. I think of cat's cradle, one of Spider Woman's gifts to the Navajo—reality remade over and over again, this way and that. A certain dexterity seems to be required in intelligence, imagination, and compassion.

I had a patient a couple of years ago who had cancer of the jaw, so the jaw was removed. An attempt was made at reconstructing his face with tissue from his thigh, but the result looked like raw meat, swollen and oozing, with a hole for a mouth. He could neither eat nor talk and breathed mostly through a tracheotomy in his neck that was always spewing sputum. I had seen him a couple of days before I was assigned to be his nurse, and his face both repulsed and frightened me. It is rare that I feel this kind of visceral reaction to a patient, however grotesque, but my eyes smarted to look at the man. I could barely stand to be in his presence, and because I had a patient who shared a room with him, I found myself quickly skirting past his bed and its half-closed curtains as if I were endangered by some sort of monster. So when I was assigned to be this man's nurse, I swallowed and smiled to myself. The reckoning. I attended first to all my other patients, so that when I approached this man's bed I would be unhurried and alert to the thread that would connect him and me. Unhurried attentiveness is what invites the grandmother in. When I hurry, she flees.

The thread was immediately obvious—small talk with his wife and changing his gown with her, which was soaked in sputum. Observing her undisguised loving and the mixture of pain, gratitude, and humor in his eyes, I said, "I'm moved to watch the sweetness between the two of you. I have a sharp eye for a good marriage because I am blessed with one. I see that you are, too."

"We celebrated our fiftieth last week," she said.

"Fifty years together!" I said, trying to imagine it. "My wife and I have been together for merely ten."

I looked at her husband, and he was weeping. If he had a mouth, I think he would also have been smiling, but his eyes were expressive enough. For the life of me, I could no longer see a monster. I saw a man who was luminous in the presence of love.

I emphasize order and beauty because those are Spider Woman's mysteries—beauty and order woven together at a deep and organic level, at the level of the heart.

One of my patients was a man named Jim. Jim was in his early forties and had a rather large brain tumor. By the time I met him, he had gone through a full ordeal—months of chemotherapy and the regimen of sleeplessness so common in a hospital. His prognosis was poor, and he knew it. He had appreciated my skills as a nurse and decided to avail himself of my skills as a *nganga*. We scheduled a date for a healing ceremony.

Although many cultures, including the Bantu, see disease as something that sometimes opens the path to initiation, there are few surviving cultures that have initiatory ordeals equal in severity to what happens routinely in a modern hospital. In traditional cultures such ordeals have always been about moving into a more profound and inclusive order. Miraculously, some patients actually find a path through the wilderness of their affliction into a deeper understanding of their place in the universe and are therefore healed. Jim was one of them. The ritual was simple enough. Jim's stay in the hospital had been so merciless that he was well prepared to go deep. Between the cancer and the almost hallucinatory psychological effects of the steroids he was taking to bring down the swelling in his brain, he was, one might say, vulnerable to the movement of Spirit. Although in truth he probably had a few months to live, we acted as if he had only a couple of hours left. Outside on our land, under the night sky, I left him alone to make closure on his life, to ask forgiveness and to forgive, if that made sense, and to reach for the deepest meanings of what it had all been about. I encouraged him toward a prayer of gratitude, because to die without gratitude makes for a miserable passage.

When I returned, we talked, and then I invoked the spirits with songs and offerings and took him in his imagination to the threshold of the village of the ancestors. By smashing a coconut, I ritualized the moment of his death. Leaving him sleeping under the moon, I had no doubt that he was among the ancestors and that his dream would be a profound one.

Some say the village of the ancestors is under the sea or deep in the forest. Mandaza said that he visited it at the bottom of the Zambezi. Jim's dream was that he was digging and digging with vigor until he came upon an ancient Jewish library filled with old and venerable books. When he awoke, I entered into the dream with him, closing my eyes as he retold the dream moment by moment so it became a shared environment, delighting with him in the awe and pleasure he felt as he reached the underground library.

After being immersed in water and taken through a ritual of rebirth, Jim headed home.

During the final few months of Jim's life, the kabbalist Rabbi Jonathan Omer-Man and I were his allies, and Jim set up camp in the sanctuary of the Word.

One afternoon, Jim's wife Anne invited me to their house. It was to be my great honor to do the final rites. Jim was ebullient, tranquil, and ready. Our conversation was often interrupted by his need to confer with invisible presences. Anne also had become quite familiar with these presences—by then they were family. Such presences seem to gather at the bedside of people who are about to cross over.

The ritual was the same as before, this time excluding the rites of rebirth. The shattered coconut I placed at the four corners of the bed. The following day Jim sank into a coma, emerging for a moment to kiss his little boy goodnight. A few hours later, he was dead.

Grandmother Spider is in love with the configuration and reconfiguration of meaning. In Jim's case, meaning was not annihilated by death; rather, death brought it to fulfillment. Beyond that, Jim's death was itself an act of healing. No one who was in touch with him during the end of his life was left unchanged. In the village of the ancestors, he had clearly learned that dying can be a fine art. His death was, among other things, a well-crafted gift to the community.

35

▼▼▼▼▼

THE SNAKE WHO PUT
MEDICINE IN MY BODY

MANDAZA: The spirits even come to me physically. I'll tell you a story about that one. One of my patients in Mutare had a dream in which he was instructed by my own spirit to take me to a mountain called Wedza. This is a sacred mountain in this country with a long history. This patient said I was being called to meet my spirits at this mountain.

So we drove to Wedza—this man and other people of the community, too. When we got there, we went straight to the top of the mountain, where we saw some old ruins. As we sat in a circle, my patient got trance possessed by his spirits and advanced toward a small cave in the ruins. I looked inside the cave from afar and saw an object that was in coils.

The spirit of this young man started meditating and invited me to come and join him in the cave. I saw that the coils were moving slightly, and I told the spirit I was afraid to come because I sensed danger there. He insisted I should come. I refused.

Immediately this young man was trance possessed by one of my warrior spirits. I recognized him. He told me to come closer because the old one was waiting for me. I had no option except to move forth.

"The old man wants to put power in your body," the spirit said. "Smell."

The smell was unpleasant. Finally he said, "Put your hand underneath this thing here." This "thing" was a big snake. We call it in Shona *rovambira*. It's quite a dangerous and poisonous snake.

I put my hand underneath the *rovambira*, and it moved. Underneath there were three herbs. I was told to eat and swallow one of them. I did that. I was told to keep the other two, and the spirits would teach me how to use them at home. After I did what I was supposed to do, the snake curled up again, and we moved away from there.

That night we slept on the mountain, and in my dreams I saw the cave again and also the *rovambira*. It was moving away from the cave, and I heard a voice say, "The old man is gone."

This is not a story. It is a true thing that happened.

36

■ ■ ■ ■ ■

THE BLACK EAGLE

MICHAEL: Alongside Grandmother Spider, Chapungu, the black eagle, is probably the main spirit who makes use of me in the hospital. Chapungu is so fierce in his kindness—a warrior, king, peacemaker, and healer par excellence. Given the nature of the terrain that a *nganga* has to walk in a hospital, I find that Chapungu is rarely far away from me.

When Mandaza placed the black eagle spirit in my body during my first initiation, I scarcely believed it and couldn't imagine what it meant. Nor could I imagine who Chapungu was. But every time I am trance possessed by Chapungu, I enter further into the sharp and swift mystery of his intelligence.

Once Mandaza and I were visiting a Tanzanian trance medium and her husband, Pio, in the slums of Bulawayo, accompanied by a few Americans whom we were introducing to the African spirit world. At one point we were all sitting in a circle in a small room. I felt the hair stand up on the back of my neck and heard the movement of large wings, the sound of feathers parting in the wind.

I did not want to be possessed. I felt a certain shyness in front of the Americans and a desire not to be exoticized by them. I glanced over to Pio, feeling a little dizzy and sick to my stomach. "Chapungu is near" was all I said.

Pio replied, "I have something just for you." He left the room and returned with a pipe and a mottled feather from the underside of Chapungu's belly. "This is only for you," he said. "Smoke it."

After taking in the harsh smoke, even before I exhaled, I felt the wind lift my arms, the spread fingers becoming black feathers. More than anything, my eyes were no longer my eyes. The sacred land of Matopos was below me, and my eyes scrutinized the landscape—a whaleback expanse of red stone, a cluster of thatched houses. At the same time, I was very much in this small room, and I would plunge down, and my wings would divide each person from the spirits that were pulling them from the path, a cut of wing here and there. Chapungu's eye for the hidden niches where confusion festers was impeccable, each person's face being the same as, continuous with, reflective of, yet separate from the terrain of Matopos.

When his work was done, the eagle departed, and I slumped over. When we walked out onto the streets, Mandaza pointed up into the sky. Chapungu was circling in the air overhead.

I do not know how to explain how it is that I could be both myself and Chapungu, both in Matopos and in this small room, or how Chapungu is very much both an eagle and also a king. Nor can I explain how it is that Chapungu's excellence in the arts of war and the arts of peacemaking are both necessary to his work as a healer. His blade cuts through conflict, but he is also a formidable defender of the helpless when they are attacked by spirits. His kindness is fierce and courageous.

I was working on a cancer ward, a long shift, a full sixteen hours. Early on, I'd noticed a teenage Mexican boy in the hallway outside a patient's room. He was wiry and tough looking, but he was also weeping. I was in a hurry, quite busy tending to my patients, but Chapungu noted the boy's grief the way he does—the bird's eye view of what exactly is happening in the territory he surveys.

A few hours later there was a commotion at the nurses' desk. Apparently this boy had gone into the staff bathroom, smeared liquid soap all over the floor, and plugged up the sink so that the room was flooded. Security was called "to scare" the boy, I was told, "just to scare him." I also found out that the boy's mother was dying and likely wouldn't live through the night.

It would have been easy to let security deal with this problem. It was possible that the boy might, in fact, be dangerous. I doubted it, but there was no telling. Aside from that, I didn't for a moment believe I had the skill to work with the situation. I had the least feel for what was going on, and I was frightened. Nonetheless, Chapungu insisted that I step forward. I vaguely remembered that courage is what happens not when one is unafraid, but when one is afraid and acts anyway.

As I said earlier, unhurried alertness seems to invite Grandmother Spider. With Chapungu, it is this gesture of stepping forward. There is a nakedness to the gesture, stark and somewhat lonely—the black eagle hovering on a current of air. As I walked to the lobby where this boy was with his large family, I thought, "Well, the worst that might happen is that I might be in a scuffle." Then, "Well, perhaps I'll make a fool of myself, but it's worth the risk."

At the moment of opening the door and seeing the boy, Chapungu flew in with unmediated kindness and insight, not for a moment afraid. I was most impressed with the precision of his language, not a word wasted.

The family had gathered around, embarrassed and apologetic for the trouble the boy had caused. They pressed around the boy, and I saw him fold into confusion. I addressed him in Spanish.

"I saw you in the hallway earlier, crying. When I was a little older than you, my father died, so I have some feeling for how difficult it must be to see your mother as she is. It's true that you messed up the bathroom because you have more feelings inside than you have words for. Am I right?"

"Yes," he said.

"And that you're not a bad person, and you will not cause any more trouble?"

"Yes."

"Some of the nurses were frightened, so they called security. I'll talk to the police and do what I can to send them away because I believe you are trustworthy." Then I looked up at the family and said, "Take good care of him. His heart is breaking," at which point the boy broke down and was held by his aunt.

As I left the room, I saw security coming down the hall. They were, in effect, ready to attack. I explained to them the conversation I had with the boy and his family. Although they were reluctant to back off, I insisted and, thank God, they relented. That's Chapungu. I'm always struck by the piercing quality of his mind, without distraction going to the heart of the situation.

The untempered blade is a source of violence. That is what I could not have understood before I was initiated. As a young man, I did much violence, not really knowing I was doing it. My sword was not only blunt, but I wielded it poorly. I was full of exuberance and bravado. Chapungu is the spirit of the tempered sword, and I am just now learning what it is to serve his wisdom.

37

▼▼▼▼▼

THE PEACEMAKER
WHO HAS NO NAME

MANDAZA: When the spirits come to me, they trance possess me, come in visions and dreams, or come physically like that old man who had those herbs. So you see, it is difficult to say how many spirits work through me. But the Peacemaker is the most powerful of the spirits. He is the one they all obey. I call him the Peacemaker that has no name.

This particular spirit can trance possess anything. It can speak from a rock, from a tree, or from human beings. The way it operates is strange, mysterious. At one point, it trance possessed my little boy Moses. So you see, it can speak through anybody. That is why it is unnamable. You cannot identify the source of this power. Michael was chosen by this spirit that he should follow the way of the Peacemaker. From this moment, don't call Michael "Michael" and don't call Mandaza "Mandaza." They are to be called peacemakers. That is what happens to a person who is ruled by this spirit. In truth, the power who is the Peacemaker we've yet to understand. So we wait.

There's something special about what my spirits, or rather, the spirits of this world, have taught me—that I should be submissive to them, that I should be their walking stick. They have taught me to love and respect all creatures, to respect and treat with compassion all the people of this world. They have even taught me to be under them—under all creatures, under all peoples of this world. Everything that lives must lead me. I am its child. They have taught me to pray so that there is peace for the world.

They have also taught me that the riches of this world are an obstacle because the more one gets in the form of the things that are of this world, the more problems one creates for oneself. We were born into this world, we found these riches here, and when we leave this world, we leave all the riches behind. The spirits have taught me to thank them for what I am.

38
■ ■ ■ ■ ■

A FOOL FOR SURE

MICHAEL: When I was last in Africa, I wanted to express my gratitude to the Shona and the Ndebele people who have truly taken me in as kin. I gathered people together. There were about thirty of us, all ages, old grandmothers and grandfathers, little boys and girls. I told them, "Ever since I came to Zimbabwe, I have been hearing over and over Christ's words, 'Do not put your light under a bushel.' Don't withhold from one another your gifts. The gift you have given me is that you have made me a *nganga*. Mandaza initiated me, but that did not make me a *nganga*. When you come to me with your suffering and your willingness to trust, my spirits come forth out of love, and they tell me how to heal. Without you, I would know nothing of what it means to be a *nganga*, and in my life I've never wanted anything more than this."

After speaking, I washed everybody's face with rainwater. "Don't hide your light under a bushel," I said. "Take very good care of each other."

A mischievous spirit had prompted me to buy a few dozen fireworks, the kind where you dangle the fuse over the lip of a bottle and send it flying in a spray of orange sparks. "God has a sense of humor," I explained.

One by one, each of us lit a firework after saying a prayer that we wanted to send to the ancestors. One woman walked up with her sister, who could neither hear nor talk, and offered a prayer on her behalf. For a second her face glowed, and she had sparks in her nappy hair. No bushel covering up that light!

CHAPTER 38

When I thought we had finished, Mandaza called to me, "Michael! You have to send up a prayer also." I had completely forgotten myself.

I looked around at the expectant faces and reached for a prayer, but I only heard silence. Each person's face was so beautiful, and suddenly I understood that I was the tribe, all of us for one second the petals of a single flower.

Squatting down, I lit the fuse. I raised my hands and chanted a prayer to celebrate the beauty of this flower—and the firework blew up in my face. I fell over and laughed until there were tears in my eyes.

In this life I am, for sure, a fool. There are worse fates. My childhood ambitions to become a saint have failed miserably. I have not become a saint, but I have learned a few things about kindness. I've learned that kindness is what one lives for. There's nothing else to live for. I've worked with dying people for over twenty years, and I know that when someone comes to the end of their life, the only thing that matters is how much they've learned to love and how willing they have been to be loved.

What I see often in America are people who will come to the end without having really learned a lot from being alive. To me this is the worst tragedy, far worse than death. The opportunity to learn to love was always there, and it was shut out. They die without ever knowing why they were alive in the first place.

The spirits have gifts, and we ourselves are gifts that the ancestors want to give to the world. The only thing to do with a gift is to pass it on. Happiness depends on being open to the gifts that are offered and to give them over with delight.

39

I AM HERE

MANDAZA: You cannot separate the ancestors from God. You can't. These are the faces of God. I agree with the Jewish scripture that says "no graven images," because what people do is create an image and then worship that image, and it becomes a God. You cannot make a God. God is not an object. If you want to see the faces of God, look at a mountain. You will really see the power of the Creator. Look at another person; you will see God. But I don't pray to that person. I pray to the power that made that person and that mountain.

Nobody is perfect. Nobody is righteous. We are all young babies. We stand up, and we fall. We stand up, and we fall.

I am not a perfect Mandaza. I am not righteous. I am just being told to say things to God's people, to God's animals. This is my message.

Over and over again I repeat, "I am here." It is all that I have to say.

CONCLUSION

*Love is the only force capable
of transforming an enemy into a friend.*

—Martin Luther King, Jr.

■ ■ ■ ■ ■

THOU SHALT NOT
MAKE ENEMIES

MICHAEL: On September 11, 2001, five years after
Mandaza and I were first initiated as twins that hot afternoon
at the Zambezi, Deena and I were in Africa. She, Mandaza,
and I were finishing up the initiation of a few Americans and
Canadians. In the evening we made a few calls back home.
Friends and family told about what had happened: mass mur-
der in New York. We gathered around CNN in a bar at a tourist
hotel adjacent to the ruins of Great Zimbabwe.

The endless repetition of the images, the planes striking
the towers, billowing smoke, people leaping to their death.
Pearl Harbor invoked, the future collapsing into the redundant
metaphor of war: so necessary, so righteous, we're told. It was
so clear that violence would proceed from this violence.

We said little that night. Mandaza has a talent for sleeping. Deena and I were simply inarticulate. I tried to imagine
what to say during the remaining two days before the initiates
returned to North America. It is not arbitrary when history
pierces into the event of initiation as did these terrorist at-
tacks. The *ngoma* of the water spirits is, after all, a peacemaking tradition.

Eventually I was able to say it: "In the Kongo some tribes
have their initiates memorize hundreds of proverbs so they
can learn to think as the ancestors do when they hold council.
Two come to mind now, one Bantu, one Jewish.

"The Xhosa elders in South Africa say, 'One's relationship
with God is best measured by one's relationship with one's

enemy.' The enemy, the one who would kill us given the chance, who we will always approach fully armed—this one is the measure of our relationship with God, the enemy who we refuse to know, the God who we refuse to know, the Immortal Stranger.

"The old rabbis said, 'The enemy is someone whose story you have yet to hear.'

"Once you are initiated, every day of your life henceforth is an initiation. Your initiation begins today. The world at large has entered initiation today."

When it was possible to fly, the initiates headed back home. However, I had purchased tickets in July to fly north to Sinai. After much debate (was it suicidal traveling in the Muslim world at such a time?), we decided to go to the holy mountain to pray for peace. On September 15, we flew to Egypt—Mandaza, Simakuhle, my infant godson Michael, Deena, and myself.

In Islam, the ninety-nine names of God connect the Nameless One to the named. Must one always be shattered—initiated—before one concedes to the One called *Ar-Rafeeq*, "the hand of God so gentle"? Or *Al-Kareem*, "God the kind"?

In African medicine, when one walks into the village of one's enemy, one pays close attention to the spirit one meets at the threshold.

"Deena, is that you?" said Mohammed as we arrived in Santa Katerina at the foot of Sinai. He recognized us from our trip five years before and had just been looking at the small album of photos we'd sent his family. His father had died recently, and when he saw the World Trade Center collapse on television, he was afraid that maybe we were dead also. As keeper of the threshold, Mohammed opened the door, conscripting his cousin to lead the camel to walk us up the back trail to the top of the mountain.

———

Long before the reign of conquest, long before the natives were Christianized or Islamicized, even long before the encampment of Moses and his refugees fresh from enslavement, Mt. Sinai was the sacred mountain of Sin, the mood god, son of the Queen of Heaven, Inanna. From the Great Mother, Tiamat, he received the tablets of the Law. "In the twelfth century BCE the Babylonian heaven was ruled by a trinity consisting of Shamash, Sin, and Ishtar, represented by the sun, moon and stars," writes Barbara Walker.

I dare say it was this Sinai that we climbed, the moon dark and the stars bright beyond telling. Here Mandaza saw Moses as a Bedouin, a keeper of goats not unlike his own people. He saw the goats running in the distance, the holiness of stone. It was here that the Peacemaker came upon us in the night.

I suppose one could imagine high drama—a thin trail of tranquility leading up the mountain, buffeted on both sides by the fires of apocalypse. After all, George W. Bush and radical Islam share a faith in redemption through apocalypse, the final drama in which the world is purged of evil and a new world order, by the grace of God, descends. Or one could imagine the Law burnt into the heart, lightning fired into stone— that drama, that violence. Nothing of the sort happened.

What happened that night was true for its gentleness—Ar-Raqeem. The desire for a cosmic vision was left at the foot of the mountain.

These days I understand the vision we were given best through my father's language, Buddhism. The Buddha of the future, it is said, is Maitreya. But Maitreya is not a person. This Buddha rather is the quality of friendship that is, in fact, an aspect of the enlightened mind. The Law, the Dharma, is realized and fulfilled in the activity of friendship in all of its many levels. Kairos, the future breaking as it must into the present moment, is the inbreaking of Maitreya. Spirit descends, friendship is inspirited, and the spirit of friendship reveals the Law: Thou Shalt Not Make Enemies Any More.

Live by this.

My arm around Simakuhle or on the back of Michael wrapped in a towel and tied to his mother. Ahead of us, Deena and Mandaza hand in hand, steadying one another on the dark trail. Sometimes visible, sometimes nearly transparent. Often only the starlight visible. Maitreya. Ar-Raqeem. The Nameless Peacemaker. After hours of walking we see the sky go to dark cobalt blue and lighter and lighter still. We arrive at the top of the mountain with the pinkening before sunrise.

The Peacemaker and the Healer are a single person, self-same spirit, and they go by one name only: Compassion. It was compassion that brought me to Africa, compassion that allowed Mandaza and me to recognize each other as twins, compassion that rose with the sun at Sinai and that has accompanied us each in our descent and the rigors of serving such a world in such a time.

A human life is small beyond telling and briefer than most of us will admit. How then does one realize compassion and live it? How to honor the modest facts of who one is and touch what is before one?

These are the questions that we live by: provocation, nourishment. Deepening only in their necessity.

As twin, Mandaza is forever beside me even as we are across the world from each other.

Not a moment to waste, especially not to waste with heedlessness and hurry.

I take refuge in my simple-mindedness, my commitment.

▼▼▼▼▼

THE HOLY SPIRIT ITSELF
WAS DRINKING

MANDAZA: It was September 11th. There was this decision that we had to make. There was a message of peacemaking, of healing the world that needed to be heard. We decided that we should go to Mt. Sinai. The spirits and ancestors were calling us there for peacemaking with the world which was in chaos at that time.

It was perhaps dangerous to travel in Arab countries just after the explosions in New York. However, we really asked the spirits to guide us, and they were with us all the time. As peacemakers, the message we got was to proceed, and we flew to Mt. Sinai immediately. We went to Mt. Sinai and were received like relatives. We were invited to go to the home of Michael and Deena's Bedouin friend Mohammed, and we listened to the dreams of his family. One little girl had many nightmares, proper *ngozi*. I cast out that spirit and had her go into the water.

We made friends instead of enemies in Egypt.

The night when we started walking to Mt. Sinai, we had to make another decision. We had to follow either the ancient path or the modern path. We decided to walk the ancient path. We had a guide, Mohammed's cousin Malik, and he brought a camel to carry our things.

We all know that the camel is a sacred animal. We started walking then. It was very special for me. This was one of the greatest calls of the calls I have undertaken. As peacemakers, the message we got was to climb, not to ride the camel.

So we started walking. It was beautiful. The life of the stars and the song of the stones were the revelation.

You know that I named one of my sons Moses. Moses is an ancestor to all enslaved people, the colonized and oppressed. We were in his presence—there was no doubt about that one. We followed him to the rock he struck where water was provided by God for the children of Israel. I could hear the songs of the water spirits gushing in that place.

I saw the presence of the holy angels there around this water, in a place of such dryness. I saw that the ancestors and the animal spirits, too, were drinking. Everything was drinking. The Holy Spirit itself was drinking.

Michael, Auntie Deena, Simakuhle, baby Michael—I felt that we were also drinking from this rock.

It was beautiful when we were walking—arm in arm with Auntie Deena, Simakuhle with our child on her back, and my *mapatya* with his hand on his godson.

So we walked that whole night, watching the signs, and seeing Moses ahead of us the whole way.

When I asked Michael how far we were from the top, he said let us go on, we will be there shortly. We were all very tired but also very determined.

When we got to the top of the mountain, I felt very fresh. I asked myself, is it true that I am sitting now with my Creator here? Because everything I saw on top of the mountain was all my Creator, all my ancestors. God was all I could see. We sat there and I started playing my *mbira*, a little beautiful music.

After Sinai, what next? Michael has gone through many initiations, before and after we met. I also underwent similar initiatory rituals in Africa. Initiations never end. They are a lifelong process.

CONCLUSION

The next steps are three in number.

The first step is ritually and with our own two hands to heal all creation.

The second step is to make peace with all creation—Mother Earth, the air, the water, the animals, the birds, and the nations, too. As peacemakers, we also receive healing from the creation in many ways. If we look after nature, nature will look after us. I say, let us look to the creatures first. We humans are so blind and cause so much suffering.

The last step is about encountering deep-rooted and more serious challenges. Some people whom we think love us will abandon us. Sometimes we will seem to lose almost everything. For us as we become more effective healers and peacemakers, problems will hit us from all angles. Despite all these challenges, the work of healing and peacemaking has to be done, until there is finally success.

To this end, we are going to usher in a new way of living: love, truth, and peace for all living things. Together we can enjoy the sweet juice, the honey, and the abundant milk of oneness.

This indeed is for all of us, not for the *mapatya* brothers alone.

EPILOGUE

How far you go in life depends on you being tender with the young, compassionate with the aged, sympathetic with the striving, and tolerant of the weak and the strong, because one day you will have been all of these.

—George Washington Carver

■ ■ ■ ■ ■

DESCENDING
THE HOLY MOUNTAIN

MICHAEL: It seems as if, since that dawn on top of Mt. Sinai, we've all been descending from the holy mountain. Mandaza has stepped forth into different communities in North America, sharing medicine with the Cowichan tribe of British Columbia and African-Americans in Los Angeles and Oakland. He has been received in India. Small communities of our work, called *Daré*, have sprung up in California, Seattle, Salt Spring Island in Canada, Cape Cod, Boston, and now Toronto. Mandaza comes in the summer to heal and offer support.

I've taken another fork in the path as I continue to descend.

James Baldwin wrote that to be truly alive is to make love with what you most fear. My lover arrived in the form of a diagnosis of multiple sclerosis.

My apprenticeship with multiple sclerosis began very slowly, retrospect being the only angle from which one might see its beginnings. I was in Africa in 1996 with Deena, introducing her to the Bantu people who had initiated and received me as a medicine man. We were in the stony waterlands of Mashvingo, southern Zimbabwe, and Deena was initiating Mandaza into the mysteries of the Hebrew letters, when I noted a garden variety of arrogance rising up in me. After all, I was "the expert," much a part of the tribal world and quite well read on Bantu anthropology. How much I wanted to interfere, be master of ceremonies! So I pulled away to a small pool of water to curl up in and prayed in the traditional way. I yielded to the field of spirits that were carrying the poetry of the moment quite without my advice. It was then that the snail parasite schistosoma slid through the skin and apparently laid eggs in the lattice of my peripheral nervous system.

That night a fever, strange but transient. Two weeks later, numbness from the waist down. And so I walked eight years with this numbness. Eighty percent of peripheral neuropathies are undiagnosable, I was told. With reluctance, accustomed to a young man's oblivious vigor, I settled into the perpetual reminder of the frailty of the flesh. I believe it made me a better nurse, a better *nganga*, a more compassionate human being.

All this started changing a couple of years after our time on Sinai, when I lost the full use of my legs. Then my apprenticeship with the sacred illness truly began. How fortunate I am that MS insinuated itself into my body at a moment of surrender and has kept such perfect faith with the teaching of surrender, and surrender, and yet again, surrender. And then there are the gifts that come in the wake of surrender.

Surrender. What do I mean by surrender? Anagarika Sujata says there is dishonesty in any mind insisting that reality occur in a specific way. MS says that healing requires a strange alliance with what one is facing. And so the way of surrender has demanded an uncompromising honesty. Not a passive acceptance, but a very active meeting.

My first serious rendezvous with the spirit of the illness was when I walked to my hermit's cave on the Big Sur coast where I'd been blessed to spend two years during my twenties and thirties in solitude and prayer. It took me ten hours to walk what would have been a one-hour hike. In my two weeks alone I surrendered my legs, not knowing if they'd return or even if I'd be able to make my way out of the ravine. Later, I surrendered my life. Undiagnosed as yet, I didn't know if that time had come. Finally, there was surrendering the fetish of certainty, accepting that God is the one who shapes what is before me. Such has been my spiritual practice during this time, and through it I have begun to taste freedom.

Occasionally!

Surrendering my legs was one thing. I was perplexed that I would be asked to do so, but with whom do I argue? Surrendering my life was a different matter, given that truculent fantasy that my life and my death are my own possessions. Deena is twenty years my senior. I've spent many years renewing the vow that I'd see her to the other side, and it would be a betrayal of both of us should fate decide otherwise. But, yes, there was that tearful moment five minutes before the New Year's kiss, when I insisted that she continue should I go first.

The third lesson from the illness was surrendering the fetish of certainty. Not long ago I was delivered vividly between worlds, flailing in rage, indulging in an orgiastic fit of self-pity. I was between lives, one life dead and gone and the next unborn, that place the Tibetans call bardo. Deena, bless her, said, "You have to let go of how you think and talk about these things." The space of the bardo echoed with "let go, let go, let go," as if to harangue. I knew that spiritually I was being called to let go of almost everything, or perhaps merely let go of any shard of imagining that I know the shape of the future.

Ah, the Fool card of the Tarot! My father gave me my first Tarot deck before he died, and I've long used it to understand my fate. Did I not see the Fool as a photograph of my soul, satchel at the end of a stick, dog nipping at my heels? Did I not always yearn to dance at the edge of the abyss?

And yet now, quite denying my years of my public and private rhetoric to the contrary, I'm seduced by certainty—the one thing I've always scoffed at with contempt. The Fool at last has the last laugh. Affectionate though he was toward the young man's flamboyance, now he places the older man's meditation cushion at the edge of the uncertainty that has become his life and says, "Sit still."

How little I've understood the Fool. A little psychosis, a bit of entertainment, half-time in the rites of surrender. I'm left with the question, stripped bare: what is the authentic and ensouled truth of the story I am in?

And so the continuing truth of initiation: the affliction itself has drawn me as a healer into a circle of healers, some alive, some spirits. This circle itself is the place of healing, the place of initiation. Healing and initiation are one and the same, the weave of many hands.

The circle of the living.

My community of friends singing, praying, drumming on my behalf as my legs began giving away, as I staggered with my walking stick. The medicine of a prayerful community: the next day I put my stick down only to use it, as Deena said, because the time had come for me to lean on the ancestors.

MS itself is the subtlest and most deft of healers, a true and vivid spirit ally, the one who knows the intimate cellular truth, undisguised, undeniable, and utterly transparent. Among the living and the spirits this Guest turns a face that is not without beauty. Who am I to argue that fate has delivered me here by accident, has called me toward the dance with this one so real in its intelligence, so relentless in its wisdom?

So there it is, descending from the sacred mountain and hearing it yet again: Thou Shalt Not Make Enemies Anymore.

Anymore.

Least of all, make an enemy of that which has taken one's flesh.

When I'd returned from Big Sur, I laughed with Mandaza on the phone. "I've been taken by snail totem! I move so slow! God is so kind in teaching me patience!"

As a *nganga* and now a former nurse, I seem to be learning and teaching about the spiritual practice of *amor fati,* loving one's fate.

AND THE STARS ARE
HER CHILDREN

In Memorium for Joyce Dube

Egg split
the cleft spread wide
but what womb where
could carry
the children of Africa and Europe?
and who is this dark mother
we call Mambokadzi, Queen
who spawns twins such as you and I
Your wife's sister maddened with AIDS
Joyce wailing in the night
you don a leopard pelt
and douse her nappy head
while I sing her a song
to the Mother of Water
We carry her to the car
to drive the dry cow path
to her mother's mud hut
Greeting us at the gate
Amai sees not only her daughter's ravaged body
but hears in the bereft stuttering
her own mother's voice
"This child I cannot heal,"
says the spirit
as Amai wraps grandmother in ancient cloth
and bows respectfully before the old one

Daughters and mothers and grandmothers
and grandmothers of grandmothers
gathering singing and clapping
You told me once the Mambokadzi was the moon
and the stars are her children
to be born into poverty
to die young in poverty
to be anguished
and possessed of an anguished spirit
What does it mean to be a healer
in such a world, my brother?
The parched earth, the long lament
the Queen herself weeping
among the children of darkness and light?
How is it that her tears
become our tears
her dust our dust?
Grandmother and the dear woman
that housed her spirit
yields to the silence
of the slivered moon
and two ragged men
one black, one white
drive the blue Peugeot
into the darkest hour
of the night

—Michael Ortiz Hill

AFTERWORD

*The world I love is in great
need of healing, and I am incapable
of healing it. Please help me.*

—"The Beggar's Prayer,"
Deena Metzger

DARÉ,
A HEALING COMMUNITY

by Deena Metzger

When my husband, Michael Ortiz Hill, first and I afterward went to Zimbabwe to be initiated by Mandaza Augustine Kandemwa, we expected our lives to be changed, but we did not expect to be educated in a way of healing that would be relevant for North Americans and actually provide a model to ease some of the most serious disruptions of modern life. On my first trip to Africa, in Johannesburg, 1997, I had this dream:

The phone rang and I answered it. No one was there. It rang again. Again no one was there. The third time a man's voice asked if I was Deena Metzger. I was astonished that anyone would find me in this hotel, as Michael and I had relied on a taxi driver to recommend lodgings. Even stranger, the deep voice belonged to an indigenous man from somewhere in South America.

I asked, "Who could possibly know me in Johannesburg?" Ignoring me, the man asked if I would carry the book made from the film, The Heart of the World, *and if I would teach the pattern. "We have identified the pattern," the man said. "We have used it, and it is effective."*

"What is the pattern?" I asked, wondering if he meant something other than the need to live in harmony with the natural world. I wanted to ask questions, and I also wanted to describe the pattern as I imagined it, but I couldn't find the words.

Then I said, "A friend of mine is with the Kogi Indians." I was mystified that I would receive this call when my friend Victor Perera, a journalist who has written about the Lacandon Maya, was possibly with the Kogi of South America. I had not talked with Victor for months, ever since he had called to say he would be visiting the Kogi to speak with them, as he had with the Maya, about their sacred wisdom traditions.

I spoke with nervousness and confusion. The man remained silent, disinterested in anything I said. When I quieted myself, he said,

"There is little time. If this contact is right, I will get the book to you tomorrow."

Still troubled by details, I began to review my plans for the next day, then realized all my plans were meaningless in the face of this possibility. Then the man asked me what I would pay for the book. Pay? It seemed an absurd question. "What do you want?" I asked, "a measly thirty dollars? If it is what you say it is, I will give my entire life to it." I was deeply unnerved as I hung up the phone.

I awakened as unnerved as I had been in the dream. I did not, could not, believe it was a dream. Though I had seen the film, I didn't know then that Alan Ereira, the BBC filmmaker, had also written a book about it and the Kogi.

It is the custom of the Zimbabwe *daré*, or "council," we were part of to tell dreams each morning. The second day we were there, I told Mandaza this dream about "the pattern" and *The Heart of the World.* After meeting him I realized that Spirit had brought all of us together to create alliances that might contribute to the healing of the world. I felt that our meeting was neither casual nor personal. It seemed remarkable that an American Jewish woman would be invited to work with a black African healer. It also happened several times that we—Mandaza, Michael, and myself, joined by Patricia Langer, a remarkable healer from Toronto—were in the company of other African healers, and we all worked with and upon each other. We were learning to yield to each other's wisdom and, in Michael's words, to "serve each other's spirits." This has been one of the great privileges of my life.

Mandaza heard the dream profoundly. He agreed it was essential to create global networks of wise, initiated people who could protect the planet and alter the destructive consciousness and behavior of those the Kogi call "the Younger Brothers." He speculated about the meaning of "the pattern." Mandaza is a humble man, but he has had many visions instructing him to collaborate with other healers across the globe.

"The pattern," we all agreed, had something to do with creating a web of connection, a circle of relationship.

After participating in initiatory work with Mandaza, Patricia and I traveled to South Africa, where we had other remarkable experiences that deepened my belief that the creation of alliances among elders of all peoples, particularly those who carry original wisdom, is the crucial work of this time. I was also instructed that alliances with the natural world are not only possible but essential.

Just as I was returning to the United States, hostilities broke out with Iraq. I was and continue to be alarmed by the global military threat. I began to propose councils of elders, calling the wisest from all traditions to sit together to see the way Spirit speaks differently but profoundly through all of us, to take responsibility together until we receive wisdom sufficient to alter the violent and greedy ways of "the Younger Brothers," who are ourselves. I thought then that these councils were one form of "the pattern" I had been instructed to teach. Here is part of what I said in the letters calling for such councils:

"The call for a global council as well as local councils of elders continues to be necessary. We must step out of our familiar ways of knowing and acting. The times are that urgent.

"I do not know if we will find ways to save ourselves, the animals, the trees, and the earth from our own destructive patterns. I do not think that any government or known system or individual will accomplish it. I am asking you to stand with me at this terrible place of not knowing without pretending it is otherwise. Let us stand here. Grieving. We are caught in a destructive system with multiple manifestations: nuclear war; biological or chemical warfare; fascism; genocide; religious, racial, and ethnic wars; terrorism; famines; urban despair; abject poverty; unprecedented incidents of mental illness, depression, psychosis among individuals, too many of them in positions of power; the decline of ethical concerns; the destruction of the rain forests; the pollution of the environment; the death of spirituality; the disappearance of plants and animals; meaninglessness—these are some of the signs of the system that acts against us.

"In contrast, there is a living net through which all beings sustain each other. As humans, we have somehow substituted the deadly net and forgotten how to be part of the living one. Realistically, how can we return? What can be done?

"We can search out each other's counsel. We can come together in unprecedented global councils, seeking wisdom outside our own traditions. We can stand together before the ruins of everything that matters without blaming each other but eager to find new ways. Even if we can do nothing but put our own threatened and weary selves before the decline that is taking our children, the calves and pups and offspring of the animals, and all the seedlings, we will know that we set our personal lives aside on behalf of all the creatures, for what matters most.

"Small circles of peers openly speaking grief, assisted when appropriate by prayer and mediation, may be blessed with understanding. Many of the elders on the planet know how to access the wisdom of Spirit and the natural world. Let us speak with each other."

The letters I wrote distributed themselves across the world, and many people were inspired to seek counsel with each other in order to find ethical and humane ways to live. Still, on many days I anguished over the world situation. Once driving along the Pacific Ocean, I found myself weeping hopelessly. Then I heard a voice within me saying,

"It is not as difficult as you think. All you have to do is put the forms in place."

"Who are you?" I asked.

"We are the Sanhedrin," the voice answered. I understood then that they were the spirits of my own tradition, a council of the wise who had advised people since the time of Moses.

During this time, I began imagining alliances with animals and other beings of the natural world. I returned to Africa the next year with Michael and two of our colleagues, Michele Daniels and Amanda Foulger. We went to Chobe in Botswana with Mandaza, where I had an extraordinary encounter with an elephant. For years I had been dreaming of elephants and their predicament to the extent that I felt called to be with them. When I saw the elephant we have come to call "The Ambassador" move toward me from half a mile away with clear determination—deliberate, conscious, intention—I realized that everything we usually think about animals has to be reconsidered. This was even clearer when the elephant approached Michael and me as we sat in the open back of a pickup truck, bowed elaborately, and then came within three feet of us to look directly in my eyes for over thirty minutes. Later as we left the park, we were unmistakably acknowledged by a half-mile line of elephants that gathered just as we were driving out.

I had approached the elephants as another holocausted people and had prayed to sit with them in some kind of council so we might make an alliance across species lines. In this elephant's presence, as in the company of Mandaza and our colleagues, I felt as if I were being informed by remarkable beings about the ways and importance of kinship.

This time when I returned from Africa, I felt compelled to establish a *daré* in my community as an outgrowth of the idea of a council of elders, following the example of the *daré* community Mandaza has established. For years I had been training healers nationally in the creative, ethical, and spiritual aspects of healing. Now it was clearly time to enact the teachings. In Bulawayo, Zimbabwe's second largest city, Mandaza has re-imagined a tribal form in an urban setting. We would do the same. *Daré* is a healing community. This means that in it, healing is the primary focus and exchange between the participants is constant and dynamic. Increasingly we have come to the radical understanding that all the members of the natural world rightly participate in community with us. Mandaza believes that "the heaviness of the spirits upon us" cause many diseases. The healer acts on behalf of spirit, opening the path between the individual and spirit and removing obstacles to the spiritual life. The ways of coming to spirit are many and can be both arduous and beautiful. Song, prayer, and ritual are as essential to the healing process as are medicine, treatment, dream interpretation, divination, and service.

In the Shona and Ndebele traditions, Spirit heals through us. "I am God's feet, I am God's hands," Mandaza likes to say. The healer's task is to become the vessel that can carry the healing spirit. In any given moment, the healing spirit passes through a room and anyone who has the capacity receives it on behalf of the community. The extraordinary healer is the one who is so devoted to the spirits that he or she carries the spirits all the time. But ultimately there is no great distinction between the healer and the one who needs healing. Just as the beggar can be the angel who calls forth our generosity, the one who is ill calls forth the healing spirits in the healer as the healer invokes them in the one who is ill. Through initiation one is both healed and empowered to bring healing to the community. The members of the community learn to sustain and heal each other. I explained this understanding in a letter inviting people to attend the first *daré*, planned to take place at Michael's and my small home in the Topanga hills in April 1999. Here is an excerpt from that letter:

"Healing is not a profession; it is a way of life. Exchange is not limited by money or one's ability, and so the sacred and beautiful are not commercialized. At this terrible time, it is essential to re-imagine art, healing, and community. These gatherings are seeds for beginnings we cannot yet conceptualize. The task is to see how we can each come forth to ease each other's suffering and concerns.

"We are trying to create a form without rules, minutes, legislation, organization, statements of purpose, grant appli-

cations, tax deductions, or agendas. We will not charge anything for *daré* or for the healing work that will take place
within it. We assume those who come will bring food and
drink and whatever else is necessary so that this day is completely successful.

"What we offer is mediation, medicine, massage, energy
work, conversation, shamanic work, curanderismo, divination,
ritual ceremony, cooking, reading, gardening, prayer, poetry,
dance, song, art, listening, silence. . . . All leading to healing.
We will call each other forth, receive from each other in the
ways we can and offer to each other what we can. To receive
what heals and to offer what sustains–this is the goal."

My Wednesday Morning Women's Healing Circle, which
had been in existence for four years, took on the responsibility for *daré* with Michael and me, and we began to meet on
the first Sunday after the new moon each month.

Many times during the *daré*s in Topanga I have felt exactly as I did during *daré* in Africa. There, after a sweat, twenty-
five or thirty of us would gather in Mandaza's small *daré* room,
one on top of the other, to listen to each other and to the
spirits speaking through us. Adults and children were packed
together, telling dreams and singing, sometimes even dancing, there among the masks, skins, baskets, herbs, and ritual
objects that make the Zimbabwean *daré* a holy place.

Here in Topanga, where thirty or so gather around the
round low table that has become a circle of animal spirits, it is
the same but different. We had to find a form that reflects the
people who live in this area of the world. You can say that,
like Mandaza, we listened to the spirits–to the many spirits
that represent the many traditions in our area–to find out

how to proceed. We hope to become adept in all the healing languages so that we can honor, regain, use, and preserve the traditions we have lost. In this way, though, we are already in Mandaza's tradition, for he has welcomed each of us from different parts of the world so warmly and has asked us to teach him the wisdom of our lineages.

As the *daré* begins, as in Africa, we meet outside because we find the presence of the land, creatures, and elements sustaining, and also because there is not enough room in the house for all the people who are usually with us in the afternoon. So far the weather spirits have been good to us.

We often use oracles to tell us how to proceed, particularly with those who have come for the first time or who are seeking relief from suffering. We are devoted to augury as a way of reading the intention of spirit or gaining guidance for the participants. We ask simple questions to orient those who come, some of whom are afflicted with serious illnesses or are suffering as so many people do in our culture from poverty, say, or loneliness or meaninglessness. We ask: Where is this person at this moment? What path is spirit laying out before him/her? What is the first step? These questions invite stories, and the stories provide a foundation for the person to find guidance for his or her life.

We never know who will come to *daré*. There are always familiar faces as well as strangers. Once a stewardess I had met on an airplane came to *daré* and received strength to challenge the medical industry, which had misdiagnosed her husband's fatal illness even while coercing him not to seek alternative treatment. Another time we were blessed by a priestess from the Yoruba tradition devoted to the goddess Yemaya. We are fortunate that there are always people from traditions other than the dominant white culture who bring with them the richness of their heritage as well as their grief. The task of the *daré* community is to welcome those who come with warmth and to discover what need has brought them here. We shape proceedings according to what the individual needs are and what is brought forth in the sessions. We pay particular attention to the direction or inclinations of Spirit in order to see how to proceed and with whom.

In the afternoon we begin to call Spirit. Someone brings out the big drum, Eve, a gift from the community to the community. Up to eight people at a time can keep the heartbeat of Eve. Other drums come out also, along with rattles and other instruments.

Introductions are made. Intentions are spoken. Someone begins. Perhaps, and according to my tradition, I will call the Holy One in Hebrew to be with us. Or Amanda Foulger may call the four directions in the shamanic tradition. Once, Mike Wimberly, an African-American bass trombonist, played music he had composed calling slaves to freedom. Or Cho Qosh Auh Ho-Oh may blow on a conch shell as did her Chumash people, indigenous to California. Richard Grossman strikes a gong or blows a didgeridoo, Netanya Selman awakens the crystal singing bowl, Sarah Vaughn picks up the clarinet, and we begin. We don't know where the music will take us. We turn to music, as Mandaza instructed us, as an essential practice because it has been a form of prayer for millennia. We call the spirits and—we are grateful—they descend.

Afterward we meet in small groups. Someone may lay on hands; several practitioners offer massage; an acupuncturist may put up her table in the grass under the eucalyptus trees while others gather around the ill people and sing into their bodies. Juliette Hanauer holds up her palms and energy pours out of them, and Ursula, Valerie Wolf's fourteen-year-old daughter, learns the way of laying on of hands.

It is difficult to explain how healing comes. Each time it is an original and wondrous event. A woman who is out of work finds a job. A brain-injured boy who did not develop past six months old celebrates his fifteenth birthday, smiles, and tries to drum on Eve. When, as so often happens, he is in pain and distressed, Michael sings a Shona prayer over him, does a little ritual work, and the boy seems eased. Another boy, ten years old, who is experiencing difficulty in school, dances like an angel and shows us his poems and drawings. The first time he came, I asked if he knew what prayer is. He said he did, and as I tied African shell ankle bracelets around him, I asked if his dance could be a prayer. He said it could, and it was. Dina Fraboni, who teaches sacred dance, moved alongside him, grateful to find a place where she can pray in her own way in community.

One man was debilitated and depressed with AIDS and is now working as an actor and landscaper and happier than he has ever been. One has come to speak his grief over his wife who had just died; two men join him in council, both having given up years of their lives to care for their dying parents. A man from Brazil stands with a walking stick and limps around the circle like old man Legba while chanting in Portuguese for his recently murdered mother. A woman wails the unmourned suicide of her brother one Passover eighteen years ago, while another comforts her and secretly grieves her own loss of her lover by chanting in Hebrew, "May this grief pass through you."

In the late afternoon, we sit in council, pass a talking stick, and address a question crucial to the community. Perhaps it concerns experiences we have had with healing, or how we live the conflict between our ethics and the impossible demands of our culture, or how we survive in a workplace that is inhuman and unethical. Or perhaps we talk about times we feel we have been corrupted and undermined our griefs, the miracles we have witnessed, how to heal each other, or what, truly, peacemaking is.

We speak spontaneously and from the heart. Month after month, as we share the deepest truths about ourselves, we change. Sometimes a person comes to speak once and never returns, yet we hear later that their lives have changed.

One man has an environmental disease; he is allergic to almost all chemicals. We speak to him as someone who is carrying a truth for us, a canary in a coal mine, showing us how we endanger ourselves with environmental devastation. He no longer feels like a pariah, even though he still must stay outside because he is made sick by the carpets, furniture, cleansers, and paints inside our houses. Someone offers him bodywork. Michael tells his cards. I counsel him. Valerie Wolf prays over him in the Native American tradition. A moving healing ritual occurs spontaneously, and at the end of it Michael kneels, singing in Shona and Ndebele, and washes his feet. Weeks later, we hear that he has found the energy to move into a house that is not infested with fungi. He is not entirely healed, but his life is better, and he is encouraged. We pray for him.

We pray for the woman who has liver cancer. She is mounted by a Tibetan Buddhist spirit of fierce compassion. Month after month, she comes to *daré*; she begins to sing after having silenced herself for over ten years. She begins to write. Her prose is passionate and lyrical. The novel she is working on proceeds. The doctor says her liver function tests can mean one of two things: she has liver cancer or she is undergoing a rapid and unprecedented healing. Suddenly she also requires surgery for cervical cancer. The community rallies around her at the hospital, attending her before, during, and after surgery. Her doctor, also a woman, is asked to imagine that every cut and stitch is an act of healing, that she is not only a surgeon but also a healer and can bring healing through her presence. The doctor says she is honored to take this on. The surgery goes well. The woman recovers well. There is no liver cancer; her liver was healing. The woman says she could not have survived this without *daré*.

We meet in small groups again. Someone takes the children for a hike. Moriyah Colaine takes the young boy who dances for a stroll in the sage-covered hills. Others meditate. People gather around the food that everyone has brought. A man from Morocco puts a delicacy he has cooked into my mouth. The atmosphere is convivial. There are two men at the sink washing dishes together. A man and a woman are making a fruit salad. People consult each other to see how to live their lives. There are healers in the room from many different traditions who have not had the opportunity to practice their art. I tell people not to hold back on their loving. This is the place where we can offer back to the community and Spirit all the gifts that have been given to us.

We meet together one last time to end the evening. Night has fallen and fog has begun moving in over the hills as if it were the ancestors returning to us. We gather in the small room, feeling comfortable even though we are all crammed against each other. Susie Green focuses healing energy onto a woman who is suffering from chronic fatigue syndrome. Someone massages someone else's feet.

Recognizing animals as part of our community, we consider a different endangered species each month. The month I took the elephant, an elephant's trunk appeared in the clouds, and birds skittered brazenly through our circle as we drummed.

People tell dreams. Gary Davidson has dreamed that a mountain lion jumped on his shoulders. We remember what Asia has just said about these animals. We think of Mandaza, who is lion totem—Shumba. We speak of this dream and others as indicating that the dreamer is undergoing shamanic initiation. Jim Deveraux speaks of what it has meant to have adopted as his son Solo, a young man from Mandaza's *daré*. Michael speaks of the violence that is tearing Zimbabwe apart before the elections. Someone begins chanting: "Africa. Africa." We all join in. The next week we hear that things are calmer there. An anonymous donor has given a sum of money sufficient to buy a tractor for the African *daré*. Eric Field says he is trying to raise tuition money for a young Masai man he met who wants to carry his people's healing tradition alongside medical training. Over the months that money is raised.

A woman who has been studying with me speaks of establishing *daré* in Boulder, Colorado. It will be different there; she has different gifts. She is a school psychologist, and she wants to incorporate the children into the council. I think of the moment when my eight-year-old granddaughter, Jamie, told a dream to the group. "I was an Indian and I didn't understand the white people in the funny clothes and hats when they came to our tents. When I woke up, I knew they were Pilgrims." She was perplexed but laughed at herself, so identified with the Indians that she was unable to understand her own language in her dream. Another young woman who has come for the first time tells a dream of being arrested by Nazis. She was certain she would be shot and left to die in a mass grave. She has suffered with this and similar dreams for almost a year. We speak of what it means to carry the enormous suffering of the twentieth century and of our people, what it means to have the grief-stricken ancestors come to us in dreams. We say we will help her carry these dreams because they are too much for any individual, especially a young woman. Several people in the room are crying. I speak to the group of the traditions in which people dream for the community rather than for themselves and of what it means to be a dreamer like Simakuhle, Mandaza's wife, who dreams the healing herbs for the well-being of the community. Jamie, with the gravity of an eight year old, turns to the young woman and gently touches her knee: "If I had a dream like that, I would get into my mommy's bed immediately and tell her my dream." "That is exactly what I did," the woman responds.

It is time to say goodnight. We sit quietly while one after another speaks the names of different people in the community who are suffering or who have suffered losses. We hold the names. We pray for them. We pray for the trees and animals that are caught in the firestorms that are raging in the western states. We sit in silence. Perhaps someone sings a song and we all join in. Then it cannot be put off any longer. We must say goodnight. Some children are carried out asleep. There are hugs and handshakes. One more time we have spontaneously woven this group of strangers and kin into a community.

Patricia Langer has organized a *daré* in Barrie, Canada, just outside of Toronto, and another in Saskatchewan. She and her students offer energy work to the ill and do healing sessions with them each week. When a child is born into the community, Patricia organizes a naming ceremony where the children call the fairies and bless the little one, who is named Megan for the Fairy Queen. Patricia also gives teachings, and a community forms itself around these new/old ideas. Her students form healing teams that attend people in the hospital, and they do ritual work for those in need. Others from San Francisco who have attended speak of forming one there. "We will do it in the park," they say. Rachel Choppin wonders how to establish *daré* in Israel as Lela Koncar considers whether something like this, no matter how limited, might be established in her country, Croatia.

There is another aspect of *daré* for which we are grateful to Mandaza. He taught us that *daré* is also a training ground where the process of healing is coincident with becoming a healer. This is what it means when Mandaza says that the spirits are heavy upon someone. It means their illness or depression is a consequence of spirit calling them—calling them to a rightful path, calling them to right relationship with the spirit world and calling them to be a healer. Without *daré* one could suffer confusion for a long time before understanding one's predicament. But in *daré* the teachings of the spirits are clear, and we learn quickly to read the signs and find our way.

Each *daré* is different because it is shaped in response to the culture and the people in it. But each is based on common principles. Perhaps we can say that, wherever *daré* exists, what we all do is "put the forms in place" and "teach the patterns."

When we told Mandaza that *daré*s were being established in North America and that some of the participants were even dreaming about him, he was amazed. "I didn't know my spirits traveled so far," he said, laughing that exuberant laugh of his which is healing in its own right.

Related Quest Titles

Luminous Essence, Daniel Santos

Mastering Your Hidden Self, Serge Kahili King

Medicine Women, Elisabeth Brooke

Native Healer, Medicine Grizzlybear Lake

The Practice of Dream Healing, Edward Tick

Spiritual Healing, Dora Van Gelder Kunz

To order books or a complete Quest catalog,
call 800-669-9425 or (outside the U.S.) 630-665-0130.